TEA

EAST & WEST

V&A Publications

TEA
EAST & WEST

edited by Rupert Faulkner

First published by V&A Publications, 2003

V&A Publications
160 Brompton Road
London SW3 1HW

V&A photography by Richard Davis of the V&A Photo Studio

Designed by Nigel Soper

ISBN 1 85177 3983

A catalogue record for this book is available from the British Library

Printed in Hong Kong

V&A Publications
160 Brompton Road
London SW3 1HW
www.vam.ac.uk

Front jacket illustration:
*Teapot and tea bowl from Tibet
(see plate 44)*

Back jacket illustrations:
*Details from plates 60, 96, 26, 56, 71, 53
and 35. Tea picker in Darjeeling, 1999.
Photo Giles Hilton.*

Frontispiece:
Detail from Interior – The Orange Blind
by Francis Cadell (see plate 84)

CONTENTS

FOREWORD

BY HENRY HOBHOUSE

A FEW YEARS AGO I APPROACHED THE POWERS THAT BE at the Victoria and Albert Museum about the idea of mounting an exhibition tracing the influence of the tea trade upon the development of European design. I had become interested in the subject in the course of researching my book, *Seeds of Change*, which shows how tea and a number of other plants have shaped the course of history. It transpired that the V&A already had plans of its own, rather more modest and somewhat different in emphasis from what I had in mind, that nevertheless dealt in part with the effects of the tea trade on western aesthetics. I was invited to participate in this project, which led to the staging of the exhibition *Ten Truths about Tea* in the summer of 2000. This book, with its stimulating variety of essays by V&A curators and outside specialists, is a fitting culmination of the project and a welcome addition to the growing body of literature on tea.

Tea was first shipped from China to Europe at the beginning of the seventeenth century. By the eighteenth century the trade in tea had grown into a massive enterprise centred on Canton (Guangzhou), where foreign merchants operated out of 'factories' – combined offices, warehouses and living quarters – on the banks of the Pearl River. Europeans arriving in China found a society far more advanced than their own. Winnowing machines for cleaning grain, seed-drills, gimbals for steadying compasses, sternpost rudders, paper, printing and even the humble wheelbarrow – these were all technologies in which the Chinese were much more proficient than the Europeans and which, in many cases, were introduced to Europe from China via the Silk Route and, later, by way of the seaways travelled by ships laden with tea and other goods.

In the realm of the decorative arts, the burgeoning of the China trade brought the porcelains, silks and lacquerwares that transformed the interiors of European houses and palaces. The pioneering of porcelain manufacture at Meissen, the rise of 'japanning' and the widespread vogue for chinoiserie, so evident in the pages of Thomas Chippendale's famous *The Gentleman and Cabinet-maker's Director*, were all direct outcomes of European exposure to the products of China and its neighbours. The tea trade also led to the design of unique sailing ships, clippers like the *Cutty Sark*, many of which were faster and more economical than the steamships of their day. It was tea, too, that was ultimately responsible for the Opium Wars of the mid-nineteenth century. These saw China diminished from a wondrous source of technology, art and learning to an object of western exploitation, almost of pillage.

One very important point about tea is not mentioned in this book, so it is perhaps legitimate for a non-academic historian to intrude the hypothesis. Before tea, there was no safe drink in southern China, all the water being infested with various forms of waterborne disease. No one before Pasteur in the late nineteenth century knew exactly why boiled water was safe to drink, but the fact is that by boiling water to make tea, the Chinese were able to inhabit areas where otherwise they would have been destroyed by illness. Gastroenteritis, dysentery and typhoid are just some of the disorders that spread in drinking water if sanitary facilities are lacking and if too many people crowd in upon each other. So, the argument runs, without tea there would not have been the kind of concentration of people that made possible the city of Canton, the European window on China responsible for the manifold developments outlined above. To this one might add that it was the declining cost and greater availability of tea in Britain that led to the shrinking of London's death rate from enteric disease during the nineteenth century. When cholera struck in the 1830s, the death rate was highest among those Londoners who were too poor to buy and drink tea.

Tea, in short, was not just a commodity traded between China and the West. It was, in accordance with the East Asian conception of food as medicine, that which sustained the health of the people of Canton, London and many other centres of population as well. Whenever one picks up a cup of tea, it should be in celebration of its life-giving qualities and its contribution, past and present, to civilized existence.

H.H. APRIL 2002

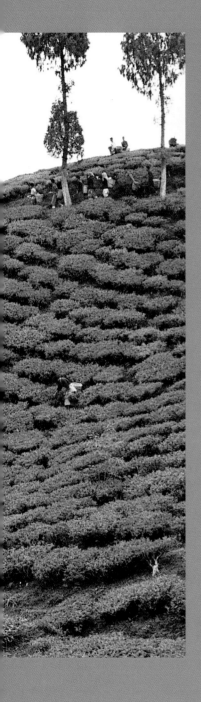

1

PRODUCTION AND TRADE

GILES HILTON

'The naming of teas is a difficult matter,
It isn't just one of your everyday games –
Some might think you as mad as a hatter
Should you tell them each goes by various names.'
AFTER T.S. ELIOT, 1888–1965

Production and trade

T HE EUROPEANS WHO ARRIVED in East Asian waters in 1514 had no idea that the future of world history would be so profoundly shaped by a plant that, unbeknownst to them, had been grown and processed in China for hundreds if not thousands of years. Initially tea was no more than an obscure herbal remedy whose existence they recorded in their diaries but to which they paid little attention. It has even been suggested that when European merchants started trading with the Chinese, they mistook the grey-coloured tightly rolled leaves for explosive gunpowder – hence the name we still use today for a particular variety of Chinese green tea.

Tea is said to have been discovered in the early part of the third millennium BC by the legendary Shen Nong or Divine Farmer. As has so often happened in the history of the human race, it was probably discovered by accident. Tea's medicinal properties, notably its ability to aid digestion and counteract the effects of alcohol, led to its adoption throughout China and its subsequent spread to neighbouring countries. By the time of the Tang dynasty scholar Lu Yu (733–804), the author of the *Chajing* or *Classic of Tea*, methods of cultivating, processing and preparing tea had reached levels of considerable sophistication.

The type of tea preparation advocated and described by Lu, which involved boiling leaves in a cauldron, was introduced to Japan in the early ninth century. This was accompanied by the establishment of tea plantations in the grounds of Buddhist temples and elsewhere. Tea drinking did not really take root in Japan until the thirteenth century, however, when Song dynasty (960–1279) methods of whipped tea drinking were introduced by Zen Buddhist monks returning from periods of study in China.

Tea drinking also spread westwards. Chinese Tang dynasty records suggest that tea was known about in Tibet by at least the end of the eighth century. As in the case of Japan, however, it was not until the Song dynasty that it started to be consumed in significant quantities. Because

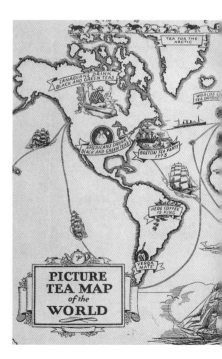

Tibet's climate is hostile to the cultivation of the tea bush, all the very substantial amount of tea drunk in Tibet had to be transported by porters and then yak caravan from where it was grown in Sichuan Province. The journey was long and arduous, and in order for the tea not to spoil or be otherwise damaged along the way, it was pressed into bricks and, for the journey through Tibet, wrapped in yak skins.

In the late seventeenth century an even longer overland route, in this case plied by camel caravans, was established between northern China and Moscow. The tea was carried in loose-leaf form until, in the mid-nineteenth century, the Russians discovered the advantages of brick tea in terms of transportability and resistance to decay. Yak caravans continued to carry brick tea into Tibet well into the twentieth century, but the building of the Trans-Siberian Railway from 1880 through to the early 1900s brought an end to the caravan trade into Russia, at least as far as tea was concerned.

The rise of tea drinking in Russia paralleled similar developments in Europe, where tea had been introduced by the Dutch in 1610 and imported on a regular basis since 1637. Its high cost meant that it was available to only a privileged few, but its popularity at court in England, for example, established it as the beverage to be drunk, in preference to other recent introductions such as coffee and chocolate, by anyone with aspirations to social acceptability. The Dutch controlled the trade in tea for most of the seventeenth century, but their position was undermined when the English East India Company began to import tea on a commercial scale in 1678.

The English East India Company's expanding interests in Asia brought it enormous profits throughout the eighteenth century. The main commodities it bought from China, trading through its warehouses in Canton (Guangzhou), were tea, silk and porcelain. Of these, tea was by far the most important in terms of both quantity and value. The Chinese, in exchange, wanted silver, which the British, by the late eighteenth century, were finding increasingly difficult to supply. Thus began the ignominious trade in opium, which ultimately led to the First Opium War of 1839–42, the occupation of Hong Kong and the forcible opening of China to British goods.

Whether it was for lack of interest or because the Chinese were successful at not divulging the secrets of an industry that was so profitable to them, western understanding of tea remained confused throughout the seventeenth and eighteenth centuries. It was believed, for example, that different kinds of tea came from different plants, and that different plants

4. *Tea pickers,*
Sri Lanka, 1891.
V&A: PH.1352–1908.

5. *Robert Fortune (1812–80). Courtesy of the Royal Botanic Gardens, Kew.*

were native to different parts of China. This aside, in the early nineteenth century the English East India Company, not content with relying on Chinese merchants for their supplies of tea, decided to go into production itself. A compounding factor in this was the rise of the Free Trade movement and the stripping of the English East India Company of its monopoly over the China trade when its charter was renewed in 1833.

In 1834 a committee was appointed to formulate a plan for the cultivation of tea in India. This came after tentative British efforts to grow tea following the discovery of indigenous tea plants in Assam in 1823. The north-east Indian tea industry was gradually established during the late 1830s and 1840s, success being achieved through the joint cultivation of imported Chinese bushes and native Assamese stock. One of the more colourful incidents of the time was the dispatching to China in 1848 of the Scottish botanist Robert Fortune (1812–80) to collect plants and information about methods of tea processing (plate 5). After travelling through China disguised as a peasant and sporting a pigtail, he returned with thousands of tea plants, a mass of equipment and a small team of experienced Chinese tea growers.

Until the 1830s tea was largely shipped in slow-moving 'East Indiamen' trading ships. Growing demand, however, coupled with a desire on the part of tea merchants to take delivery of the new season's tea as soon as possible led to the emergence of the clipper, sailing ships which 'clipped' by half the long journey from China to Europe and North America. The first clippers were built in the USA and sailed between China and East Coast ports such as Baltimore, Boston and New York. During the 1850s clippers also sailed out of San Francisco on the West Coast. When the last of the Navigation Acts was repealed in 1849, allowing American and other foreign vessels to ship goods directly into Britain, competition forced the British to start building their own clippers. The clipper trade reached its zenith during the 1860s, a particularly famous moment being recorded on the night of 6 September

1866, when the *Aerial* and *Taeping* arrived in London within thirty minutes of each other, 99 days after leaving the Chinese port of Fuzhou (plate 6).

Just as the building of the Trans-Siberian Railway spelled the end of the Russian caravan trade, the rise of the steamship, coupled with the opening of the Suez Canal in 1869, brought a close to the era of the clipper. At the same time China's supremacy in the world of tea was being increasingly challenged. 1886, for example, was the last year in which China headed the list of tea exporters to Britain, home of the world's thirstiest tea drinkers, and in 1900 it was overtaken by India in terms of overall production. This was also the period when tea growing began to spread beyond East and South Asia to Africa and other parts of the globe.

At the start of the twenty-first century tea is grown in a total of 51

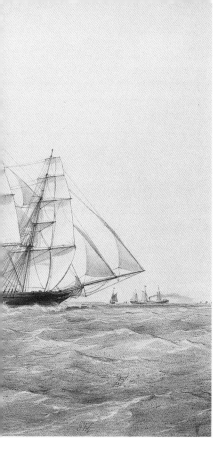

6. The Great China
Race, *lithograph, by*
T.G. Dutton, 1866.
Courtesy of the
National Maritime
Museum, Greenwich.

countries. Global production has more than doubled since the early 1970s to reach a current figure of over three million tonnes per year. This compares with a little under five million tonnes per year for coffee. India, China, Sri Lanka, Kenya and Indonesia are the world's largest producers of tea. They are also major exporters. India and China, with their enormous populations, top the list of consumers, after which come the United Kingdom, Japan – also a substantial producer – and Russia. Turkey, in sixth place as both producer and consumer, is wholly self-sufficient. In the USA, which comes eighth in the list of consumers, the amount of tea drunk is less than ten per cent of that of coffee. Iran, in ninth place as both producer and consumer, imports about a third of its tea.

China, the birthplace of tea, has always been a major consumer of the beverage. In India, on the other hand, it has only been since the early twentieth century, long after the country became a major tea growing region, that tea drinking has become popular. The implementation of the India Tea Cess Act of 1903, whereby growers paid tax to be used specifically to promote sales of Indian tea, was an important factor in this. When Lord Curzon, the Viceroy of India, was presented with a draft bill by the General Committee of the Indian Tea Association, Calcutta, he insisted that the wording be changed from 'pushing the sale and increasing the consumption of Indian tea in countries other than the United Kingdom', to 'promoting the sale and increasing the consumption in India and elsewhere of teas produced in India'.[1] Thus began a concerted campaign to promote tea drinking on the Indian subcontinent. While the British way of infusing tea in a teapot is regarded as the correct and proper way of preparing tea, most tea in India is made by adding tea leaves to a mixture of milk and water boiling in a metal pot or kettle. Sugar is added either to the boiling mixture or to individual servings of tea. Tea prepared in this way is known as *chai* or, when spices such as ginger, cloves or cardamom are added, *masala chai*. An interesting variation, popular in Kashmir, is *kahwa*. In this case, no milk is used and the flavour is enhanced by the addition of rose petals.

Despite the many developments that have taken place in countries like India, including the introduction in the mid-nineteenth century of powered rollers and other forms of machinery designed by Victorian Britain's ablest engineers, China remains the ultimate source of knowledge about tea processing. Even today China produces the greatest variety of teas in the world, ranging from the ordinary to the sublime. Chinese tea gardens tend to be small family-run affairs only a fraction of the size of African, Sri Lankan and Indian plantations, with their complements of hundreds or thousands of workers.

The success of Chinese tea gardens derives from their use of traditional bamboo mats and baskets to shape the hand-rolled leaves as they are dried over charcoal fires burning in earthenware crocks. Mechanization is found to some degree at tea factories formerly owned by the state, but even there one still finds workers sitting at large tables sorting leaves by hand. The continued use of traditional methods in China contrasts with the more modern processes used in other countries, the majority of which have come to tea growing relatively recently.

There are three main categories of tea – green, oolong and black. They are all made from the leaves of the same bush, the *Camellia sinensis*. The original Chinese variety, which is grown in China, Japan and the older gardens of Darjeeling, is relatively delicate. The Assam variety, discovered by the British in 1823, is more robust and is the one planted elsewhere in the world. The essential difference between green, oolong and black tea is the degree to which the leaves are allowed to ferment or oxidize, green tea being unfermented, oolong tea being partially fermented, and black tea being fully fermented. Fermentation is what happens to leaves in autumn, when they are deprived of sap and begin to turn brown. In tea production artificial rolling of the leaves releases the juices and enzymes that cause fermentation, which is then controlled and arrested by the application of heat.

7. *Firing tea,*
watercolour on
paper, Chinese,
about 1780–90.
V&A: D.1077–1898.

Green, oolong or black, the vast majority of tea consumed today is prepared from loose-leaf tea. Powdered tea made from the best grades of Japanese green tea is still drunk in Japan, primarily in the context of the tea ceremony, and there is also a continuing market for cake and brick tea, made by compressing processed tea leaves in moulds, particularly in the Tibetan region. The quantities involved, however, are minute. A development of the 1980s onwards has been the processing of tea leaves to produce instant tea. This has yet to catch on in a substantial way, but considerable investment in new factories is currently being made in both Africa and Sri Lanka. Japanese manufacturers have also been experimenting with non-instant but nevertheless soluble forms of green tea.

Chinese green tea is dried as soon as possible to prevent fermentation. The leaves are loosely tossed in a bamboo basket over a fire to remove moisture and to render them pliable. They are then rolled around a firing basket or pan to give them shape as they dry (plate 7). This results in a leaf with a greyish green colour which, when infused, produces a light and refreshing brew with a touch of sweetness and a gentle dry astringency.

White tea is a rare and much sought after variation made from the unopened shoots of specially pruned bushes picked during a short period in spring. The silvery white tips are processed in the same way as green tea except that they are lightly steamed to prevent them changing colour. These are then worked into various shapes such as tightly rolled pearls, long straight spikes, or bundles tied with thread. They produce an almost colourless infusion which, because of the very high concentration of sap in the new shoots, is recognized as particularly healthy.

In the case of Japanese green tea, fermentation is prevented not by warming in baskets but by heating with steam. The resulting leaf is much greener than its Chinese equivalent. The Japanese tea industry is far more mechanized than in China, large sums of money being invested in rollers,

8. *Drying tea, watercolour on paper, Chinese, about 1780–90. V&A: D.1076–1898.*

9. *Monkeys picking wild tea, watercolour on paper, Chinese, about 1780–90. V&A: D.1075–1898.*

sifters, driers and graders. This allows the Japanese to pick their bushes every four to six weeks, collecting shoots of up to twenty centimetres long, rather than having to pick newly sprouted tips weekly as in other tea producing countries. Japanese green tea has a fine, pure aroma, but without the sweetness of Chinese green tea. There are many high-quality grades, but the consistency resulting from the technological approach taken to tea manufacture in Japan means that there is less of the individuality to be found among Chinese teas.

With semi-fermented oolong tea, specially selected leaves are allowed to wither naturally, sometimes in direct sunlight (plate 8), and are then tossed in bamboo baskets to bruise their edges. The leaves are repeatedly rolled and separated over a light heat, their outer parts being allowed to ferment but their centres being kept green. The process is carried out in the course of a single day. Oolong teas are a speciality of Fujian Province and also of Taiwan, where migrants from Amoy (Xiamen) settled in the early nineteenth century. They are characterized by a distinct nuttiness combined with delicate floral overtones. Perhaps the most famous variety, which comes from China, is the so-called 'monkey picked' style, which is reputed to have been picked in the past by trained monkeys from wild self-sown tea bushes (plate 9).

Compared with oolong tea, whose production requires the utmost of skill, black tea may seem relatively simple to manufacture. Nevertheless, attention to detail is essential if a high-quality product is to be made. The first step is the withering of the freshly picked leaves on large flat perforated trays, through which air, sometimes warmed, is blown

10. *Withering tea,
Sri Lanka, 1891.
V&A: PH.1376–1908.*

11. *Man working
a tea roller,
Sri Lanka, 1891.
V&A: PH.1367–1908.*

12. *Tea grading
machine, Darjeeling,
1997. Author's
photograph.*

(plate 10). After the leaves have lost 60 per cent of their moisture, which usually takes about sixteen hours, they are pliable enough to be rolled. As the leaves are fed into the roller they are compressed and broken up (plates 11 and 13). The extent of the rolling varies according to the grade of leaf required. Fermentation starts the moment the leaf is picked, but this is greatly accelerated by the release of juices and enzymes during rolling. The leaves are left to ferment for about six hours, during which they turn completely brown. The leaves are then fired on hot air conveyors which dries them and stops further fermentation. Once they have been fully dried, the leaves are passed through a grading machine to separate them into different sizes (plate 12).

For much of the nineteenth and early twentieth centuries, as new countries established plantations and worked towards attaining standards acceptable to the burgeoning number of tea drinkers around the world, developments in tea were producer-led. The experimental nature of this period ensured the availability of a rich variety of styles and flavours. Since then developments have been mainly consumer-led, which has resulted in increasing uniformity and standardization. The huge increase in the use of tea bags in recent decades has led tea factories to produce more and more small-leaf tea. This makes a strong and darkly coloured brew which is devoid, however, of the delicate and sophisticated flavours that can be obtained from large-leaf teas. The 1970s supermarket wars, when price rather than quality became the key criterion, also had a deleterious effect. Many tea drinkers despaired of finding good quality single-estate leaf teas and switched to Continental-style flavoured teas or caffeine-free fruit and flower infusions.

As we enter the new millennium, however, the days of high-quality tea look brighter. Just as the 'real food' movement with its championing of organic farming and small-scale production has built up a sizeable momentum in recent years, there has been a noticeable rise in demand for high-quality teas from discerning customers throughout the world. Growers in Darjeeling and elsewhere have been responding to this enthusiastically, selling their products not through the traditional channel of the tea auction, but directly to tea merchants sensitive to the requirements and tastes of their customers. While the effort required to produce such teas will preclude them from ever being made in large quantities, the anticipation is that, as has been the case with fine wine, a market will develop that is sufficiently robust to guarantee the future of the true art of tea making.

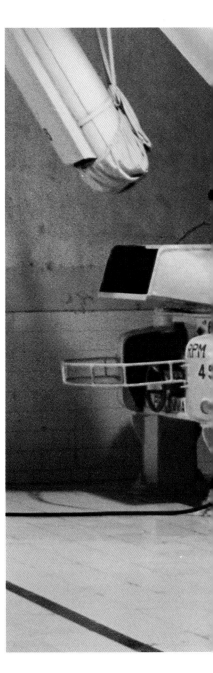

13. *Tea rollers, Darjeeling, 1997. Author's photograph.*

(Overleaf)
14. *Tea pickers, Darjeeling, 1999. Author's photograph.*

2

CHINA

MING WILSON

'The country cannot do without a ruler for one
single day. The ruler cannot do without a cup
of tea for one single day.'
EMPEROR QIANLONG, R. 1736–95

CHINA

T HE DISCOVERY OF TEA is traditionally attributed to Shen Nong or the Divine Farmer, who lived, according to legend, in the third millennium BC. He tasted thousands of herbs in order to discover their properties, caring little for his own safety, and in the process chanced upon the tea plant. An alternative story, rather less widespread, is that the beverage was discovered when a few leaves accidentally fell into a pot of boiling water. The fact is, however, that tea cannot be made from unprocessed leaves. The second story is also unpopular because it undermines the importance of one of China's national heroes.

Despite its early discovery tea was not drunk during the Shang dynasty (*c.*1700–1050 BC), when writing was invented and historical records began. Archaeology has brought to light a large quantity of exquisite bronze wine vessels dating to the twelfth and eleventh centuries BC, but none for tea drinking. This concurs with literary evidence suggesting that wine was the common drink of the time. Zhou dynasty (*c.*1050–221 BC) records show that there were two court officials in charge of tea, but that this was in connection with funerary rituals rather than consumption of tea by the living.[2]

The Chinese literati always lauded wine drinking. They believed that one's mind was at its most creative when one was inebriated. This did not stop them, however, from drinking tea. Indeed, for tipsiness to induce creativity, they had to stay sober at times. Tea, they found, was helpful in this respect.[3] Buddhists, who abstained from alcohol entirely, were another important group of tea drinkers.

By the time the scholar Lu Yu was born in AD 733, tea drinking was well established among all classes of Chinese society. Lu gained immortality as the author of the world's first treatise on tea, the *Chajing* or *Classic of Tea*.[4] While his contemporaries mixed spring onions, ginger, dates, orange peel and peppermint with their tea, he argued eloquently for the drinking of tea on its own. The many detailed instructions given by Lu include entries about the importance of choosing the right water and fuel.

(Previous pages)
15. *See plate 26.*

On water: 'The best is water from mountain streams, the next best is water from rivers, the least desirable is water drawn from wells.'

On fuel: 'The best is charcoal, the next best is strong-burning firewood such as mulberry, ash or paulownia. Do not use charcoal that has previously been used to grill meat or fish. Do not use resin-rich wood such as cypress, cassia or juniper. Never use wood from discarded furniture.'

For the making of tea, the *Chajing* stipulates a total of 25 utensils: a stove, an ash pan, an iron rod to break the charcoal into small pieces, fire-tongs, a cauldron, a frame to support the cauldron, bamboo tongs to hold the tea cake during roasting, a paper bag to hold the roasted tea cake, a grinder, a brush, a sieving box, a measuring spoon, a wooden water-bucket, a water filter, a ladle, stirring sticks, a salt jar, a jar for boiled water, tea bowls, a basket for holding ten tea bowls, a wash basin, a lees jar, a cleaning cloth, a cabinet to hold all the utensils and, finally, a basket to hold the cabinet.

The fact that Lu specified a basket for ten tea bowls indicates that tea drinking was a social event. Given the complexity of what was involved, the preparation of tea was clearly something to be done at leisure and in the company of friends. One can visualize Lu in a study with five or six fellow gentlemen. A servant would start the stove. The roasting of the tea cake would have been too important a task to leave to a servant and would have been done by Lu himself. Water was brought to the boil and salt was added. At the second boiling Lu ladled out some of the water and set it aside in a jar. Using the stirring sticks he stirred the boiling water in the cauldron and mixed in the freshly ground tea. As soon as a froth appeared, and just before the liquid spilled over, he poured the water previously ladled out back into the cauldron to lower the temperature. The tea was then served.

The *Chajing* lists a wooden bucket as the container for stream water. There exists today a large quantity of stoneware ewers which would have served the same purpose. The ewer in plate 17 was made in the Changsha kilns in Hunan Province. Changsha wares are typically decorated with appliqué motifs highlighted in iron-brown under a beige or buff-coloured glaze.

Lu considered green tea bowls to be the best. White bowls were felt to be unsuitable because they made the tea look red. Yellow and brown bowls were similarly frowned upon because they made the tea look purple or black. Green bowls, on the other hand, enhanced the colour of the tea in just the way required. The preferred shape for a tea bowl was one with shallow rounded sides and a straight upright rim, the capacity being no more than half a *sheng* or 300 millilitres of water. Although its glaze has deteriorated somewhat after centuries of use, the bowl in plate 17 matches Lu's specifications almost exactly.

The white lidded jar in plate 16 dates from after Lu's time, but is of a kind he would have approved of for a salt jar. It was produced in the Ding kilns in Hebei Province in the eleventh century. One can imagine that salt jars were kept far away from the kitchen to prevent contamination by the grease and smell of cooking.

The lees jar on Lu's list is described as being quite large. It was used as a receptacle for the leftover tea when the tea bowls were being cleaned. Lu's contemporaries would have used not only lees jars but also spittoons like the

16. *Jar and lid, stoneware, Ding kilns, 11th–12th century. V&A: Circ. 38–1934.*

17. Ewer, stoneware,
Changsha kilns,
7th–8th century.
V&A: C.833–1936.
Tea bowl, stoneware,
Changsha kilns,
9th century.
V&A: FE.126–1978.

example in plate 18, into which they would have spat the spring onions and other solids they mixed with their tea.

The last two items on Lu's list, the cabinet and basket, suggest that tea drinking also took place outdoors. Lu and his friends would roam the mountains, followed by servants carrying the tea-making equipment. When they stumbled upon a clear running stream, they would stop and make tea, using branches found on the spot as fuel. Poems would be composed, and ideas exchanged and debated.

18. *Spittoon, stoneware, Changsha kilns, 10th century. V&A: C.31–1952.*

19. *Ewer, qingbai type porcelain, Jingdezhen kilns, 11th–12th century. V&A: C.112–1929.*

(*Overleaf*)
20. Selling Tea, *ink and colour on paper, by Yao Wenhan, 18th century (after a 13th-century version). Courtesy of the National Palace Museum, Taipei.*

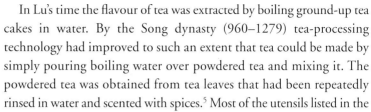

In Lu's time the flavour of tea was extracted by boiling ground-up tea cakes in water. By the Song dynasty (960–1279) tea-processing technology had improved to such an extent that tea could be made by simply pouring boiling water over powdered tea and mixing it. The powdered tea was obtained from tea leaves that had been repeatedly rinsed in water and scented with spices.[5] Most of the utensils listed in the *Chajing* were no longer required. Making tea had become very easy. Much to the delight of travellers and others, stalls selling tea at the cost of only a few coins a bowl appeared at roadsides and market places (plate 20).[6]

In the eleventh century an official in charge of sending tea to the court recorded how tea drinking had become a game in many parts of the country.[7] Five or six people would each place powdered tea in a bowl, over which boiling water was poured. Using a bamboo whisk, each person would try to whip up as much froth as possible. The criteria for winning were that the froth should be rich, that it lasted for a long time, and that the powdered tea had dissolved completely. If the froth disappeared quickly or some of the tea powder remained visible in the bowl, the contestant would be considered a failure.

Not all tea drinkers indulged in this game, but everyone liked to see a rich froth. Tea wares of the period reflect this change in tea-making practices. Ewers had long spouts to ensure a steady and even flow of water. The bluish white *qingbai* glaze on the example in plate 19 was a speciality of the kilns of Jingdezhen, a town in Jiangxi Province in central southern China that emerged as an important porcelain manufacturing centre in the tenth century. Since the porcelain would not have withstood being placed directly on a stove,

boiled water would have been transferred into the ewer from a cauldron.

Black or brown tea bowls now became extremely popular. Lu had criticized brown bowls because they made the tea look black. When people started to drink whipped tea, however, dark bowls were preferred because they enhanced the whitish colour of the froth. In the tea-growing regions of Fujian Province in south-eastern China, coarse-grained dark-bodied stoneware bowls began to be made at the Jian kilns. With their thick heat-retentive walls, these soon found favour among *Chan* (Zen) Buddhist monks, who drank tea to help them stay awake while they practised meditation but who considered white-bodied porcelains from Jingdezhen and elsewhere too refined for their austere taste.

Rustic though they might seem on first sight, Jian ware bowls are in reality highly sophisticated products. The potters manipulated the glaze mixture and the firing and cooling processes to create a wide variety of decorative effects. Depending on their patterning the bowls were called 'hare's fur bowls' (*tuhao*; plate 21), 'partridge feathers bowls' (*zhegu ban*) and other figurative names. They are particularly distinguished by a thick welt of treacle-like glaze gathered above the foot. This is the result of the glaze being very thick and fluid, and having a tendency to run down from the rim. Whether this was achieved by design or accident is difficult to

21. *Left: Tea bowl, stoneware, Jizhou kilns, 12th–13th century. V&A: C.999–1922. Right: Tea bowl, stoneware, Jian kilns, 12th–13th century. V&A: C.841–1936.*

ascertain, but this feature has definitely added to the attractiveness of Jian ware bowls.

Competing with Jian wares were the stoneware products of the Jizhou kilns in neighbouring Jiangxi Province. Jizhou ware bowls are particularly renowned for their paper-resist designs. Patterns in the form of birds, flowering branches and calligraphy were cut out in paper and affixed to the interior of the bowl. Careful preparation and application of the glaze resulted in the paper-cut design appearing, as it does in the example in plate 21, silhouetted against a streaked, cream-coloured ground.

Bowl-stands like those in plate 22 were widely used from the eleventh century onwards. In keeping with the Chinese tendency to attribute any new discovery to older times, it is said that the bowl-stand was invented by a noblewoman in the eighth century.[8] Finding a tea bowl too hot to hold, she put it on a saucer; and to stop the bowl sliding on the saucer, she put wax around its foot. Whatever the truth of this story, we know for certain that the blue ceramic bowl-stand was made for Emperor

22. Left: Bowl-stand, stoneware, Ru kilns, 1090–1127. V&A: FE.1–1970. Right: Bowl-stand, lacquer on silk core, dated 1034. V&A: W.3–1938.

Huizong (reigned 1101–25) at the imperial Ru kilns in Baofeng, near the capital of Kaifeng in Henan Province. It is completely covered with a finely crackled light blue glaze and was supported during firing on a small number of tiny spurs. The high failure rate of Ru wares, the result of the emperor's desire to see the minimum number and size of spurs used, is responsible for the fact that only 150 examples of Ru ware have survived worldwide. Of less illustrious origins, but equally elegant, is the lacquer bowl-stand. Lacquer is the sap of a tree, *Rhus verniciflua*, used to provide a protective and decorative coating to vessels made of wood, bamboo and other materials. This example, whose core is made of stiffened silk, is extremely light. It is inscribed with the name of a lacquer workshop in Changsha, Hunan Province, together with a cyclical date corresponding to 1034.

The changeover from whipped tea to steeped tea, the type of tea found in China today, took place gradually. Judging by contemporary paintings and the quantity of extant teapots, the steeping method became well established during the sixteenth century.[9] Non-fermented green tea, semi-fermented oolong tea and fully fermented black tea each found favour with different clientèles. Developments in processing methods went hand in hand with the increasing use of added flavours and fragrances, jasmine being the best known of these.

The advent of steeped tea drinking also resulted in the rise to prominence of 'purple sand' (*zisha*) teapots from Yixing, a small town located a little way inland from Shanghai. The term 'purple sand' refers to the locally occurring clay, which fires to a variety of rich brown colours. Tea connoisseurs have traditionally praised Yixing teapots for the way in which they 'drive away the smell of boiled water but do not rob the tea of its aroma'.[10] Silver teapots, though more expensive, were thought to be in poor taste.[11] In the spirit of Lu Yu, gentlemen scholars of the late Ming (1368–1644) and Qing (1644–1911) dynasties contrasted the spiritual loftiness of tea drinking with the hedonism of lavish dinner

23. Leisure Talk in the Palace, *ink and colour on paper, by Chen Hongshou (1598–1652). On the man's lap rests a lute in a silk bag. Courtesy of the Shenyang Palace Museum.*

parties. As in plate 23, tea drinking was often associated with music, a skill not to be found among the uncultured.

Because of the elevation of the context in which their teapots were used, the potters of Yixing enjoyed a higher social status than their counterparts elsewhere. Since the clay needed no glazing, the desirability of their pots depended on the skilfulness and artistry of their modelling. Top-ranking potters teamed up with scholars, who either designed the pots or embellished them with poems. Both the potter and the calligrapher would affix their seals to the pot, a privilege regularly enjoyed by calligraphers but rarely afforded to craftsmen. Yixing teapots, both old and new, have, as a result, remained prized items to this day.

Sixteenth- and seventeenth-century Yixing teapots are generally quite large. In the eighteenth and nineteenth centuries, however, pots of different shapes and sizes were made to suit different requirements (plate 24). People who liked to finish each brew in one sip, for example, would use small teapots in conjunction with small teacups. Given the impracticality of placing teacups, especially smaller ones, on bowl- or cup-stands, saucers came to be used instead (plate 25). Chinese potters

24. Left: Teapot, stoneware, Yixing kilns, by Yang Pengnian, 1800–25. V&A: C.47–1968. Right: Teapot, stoneware, Yixing kilns, by Shao Jingnam, mid–19th century. V&A: FE.1–1984.

25. Cup and saucer, porcelain, Jingdezhen kilns, late 17th century. V&A: C.34–1909.

probably learned about saucers from their European customers, who ordered large quantities of tea wares from China and Japan from the seventeenth century onwards. The use of handles, which became commonplace on European ceramics during the eighteenth century, never caught on in China and most teacups continued to be made without them.

In the eighteenth century a new type of tea bowl with matching lid came into existence (plate 26). Best described as 'guest tea bowls', these performed a different function from small teacups and were used by civil servants and merchants to serve tea to the many business guests who called on them. When such calls became too numerous the host found it more convenient to serve tea in lidded bowls. By brewing the tea directly in the bowl, the teapot could be dispensed with and time and effort saved. The serving of tea on such occasions was purely a formality. The visitor seldom knew the host well and the purpose of the visit was definitely not to appreciate the subtleties of tea.[12] Lidded tea bowls were also used in tea houses, where the atmosphere was far more relaxed. Waiters would continually refill the bowls with boiling water, and

26. Tea bowl and lid, Famille Rose type porcelain, Jingdezhen kilns, 1821–50. V&A: 440–1872.

customers could linger for as long as they liked.[13]

During the turbulent years of the 1960s and 1970s tea drinking was stripped of all its attendant niceties. Most people drank tea simply to quench their thirst. With the growth of the economy since the 1980s, however, the Chinese have once again begun to spend liberally on both tea and tea utensils. Not only do they demand the best in terms of taste and aroma, they are also interested in the appearance of what they are drinking. In Shanghai, for example, one can find jasmine tea shaped like a bud that turns into a fully opened chrysanthemum when steeped in a lidded bowl. In scenic Hangzhou there are elegant tea houses designed specifically for the appreciation of fine tea. At the opposite end of the spectrum there are the bustling tea houses of Guangzhou (Canton), where tea plays a subsidiary role to the serving of snacks known as *dimsum*.

The use of milk and sugar has always been considered a western practice, since that was how tea was drunk by westerners in China in the nineteenth century. Like other foreign drinks such as Coca-Cola and coffee, milk tea is the choice of the young. The demands of their busy lifestyles are increasingly met by products such as 'three-in-one' sachets containing instant tea mixed with sugar and powdered milk. The tea bag is another foreign import that is gaining popularity in China. Since the Chinese have a long tradition of brewing tea directly in the cup, its adoption has been less revolutionary than elsewhere. The driving force, as in other countries, has been convenience, the very least of Lu Yu's considerations twelve hundred or so years ago. The 25 utensils listed in the *Chajing* can still be seen in China today, but only in the context of performances designed to remind the world of China's contribution to global tea culture.

3

JAPAN

RUPERT FAULKNER

'There is a subtle charm in the taste of tea which makes
it irresistible and capable of idealism … it has not the
arrogance of wine, the self-consciousness of coffee, nor
the simpering innocence of cocoa.'
OKAKURA KAKUZŌ, 1862–1913

Japan

(Previous pages)
27. Detail from plate 29.

ENGELBERT KAEMPFER (1651–1716), the German physician who
served at the Dutch East India Company's factory on the island
of Deshima in Nagasaki Harbour from September 1690 to
November 1692, wrote about Japanese tea drinking in his *History of
Japan* in the following terms:

> The Tea, as it is taken inwardly, is prepared in … [three] different
> ways. The first is used by the Chinese, and is nothing else but a
> simple infusion of the Tea-leaves in hot-water, which is drank as
> soon as it hath drawn out the virtue of the Plant. The same way of
> drinking Tea hath been also introduced to Europe, and is now so
> well known to every body, that it is needless to add any thing about
> it. The other way, which is peculiar to the Japanese, is by grinding:
> The leaves are a day before they are used, or on the same day,
> reduced into a fine delicate powder, by grinding them in a hand-
> mill … This powder is mix'd with hot water into a thin pulp,
> which is afterwards sip'd. This Tea is called … thick Tea … and …
> is that which all the rich people and great men in Japan daily
> drink. … There is still a third way of making the Tea by a perfect
> boiling, which goes further than a simple infusion, and is used by
> the vulgar and Country people, who drink of it all day long.[14]

Elsewhere in his remarkable account of late-seventeenth-century Japan,
Kaempfer comments on how the '*Tsianoki*, that is the *Tea-shrub*, is one
of the most useful Plants growing in *Japan*' and that the 'common drink
of the Japanese is brew'd of the larger leaves of this Shrub', while 'the
young and tender leaves dried, powder'd and mix'd in a Cup of hot water
in to a sort of Soup, are drank in houses of people of quality before and
after their meals'. He also notes how 'it is the custom of the Country to
present friends that come to visit them, with one or more dishes of Tea,
both when they come and go'.[15]

28. *Boiled tea drinking
in the grounds of the
Kameido Tenjin Shrine,
woodblock fan print, by
Utagawa Hiroshige,
1843–7.
V&A: E.537–1911.*

The last of the three types of tea drinking described by Kaempfer is illustrated in plate 28, a mid-nineteenth-century depiction of the Kameido Tenjin Shrine in the eastern part of Edo (modern Tokyo), which shows boiled tea being served to clients resting on benches under an expansive trellis of purple-flowering wisteria. It can be seen how the woman on the left is carrying a tray of cups filled from the cast-iron cauldron that is partially obscured by the pine tree in the centre.

Lack of evidence makes it difficult to plot the history of this kind of tea drinking, but it is known that by the start of the fifteenth century low-grade tea was being sold for commoners' consumption in the immediate vicinity of the Tōdaiji Temple in Nara.[16] It is also known that boiling was used to prepare decoctions and infusions from other herbal matter such as mulberry leaves, the virtues of which were discussed as early as the beginning of the thirteenth century in the *Kissa Yōjōki* (*A Record of Drinking Tea for Good Health*), written by Eisai (1141–1215), the founder of the Rinzai sect of Zen Buddhism. This being the case, it is not in fact certain whether *senjicha*, the term for boiled tea that appears, for example, on the sign to the right of Hiroshige's depiction of the grounds of the Kameido Tenjin Shrine, necessarily indicates the use of tea in the proper sense. What is interesting, however, is that if one goes back to the earliest records of tea drinking in Japan, one finds that brick or cake tea (*dancha*) of the sort described by the Chinese Tang dynasty scholar Lu Yu in his eighth-century *Chajing* (*Classic of Tea*) enjoyed a brief period of popularity at the court of the Japanese Emperor Saga (reigned 810–23). The fact that the preparation of *dancha* involved the same kind of boiling as *senjicha* leads one to speculate that even the humblest of Japanese tea drinking traditions may have had its origins in the elitist court practices of the early Heian period (794–1185).

Whipped tea, the second type of tea drinking described by Kaempfer, is made with powdered tea (*matcha*). This is put into a tea bowl to which hot water is added, and an evenly textured suspension of tea powder in

秋山武右エ門

東京日本橋本町三丁目九番地

29. *Making thick tea*
(koicha) *during the tea
ceremony, woodblock
print, by Mizuno
Toshikata,
1890–1900.
V&A: E.3131–1905.*

water, which is drunk in its entirety, is made by mixing
with a small bamboo whisk. Kaempfer specifically refers
to thick tea (*koicha*). This is used in distinction to thin
tea (*usucha*), wherein less tea powder and more water are
used. A kneading movement is used in the making of
thick tea, which is dark green in colour and has a
consistency similar to the residue in a cup of Greek or
Turkish coffee, whereas with thin tea a more vigorous
whipping action produces a paler green liquid with a
light surface froth.

Whipped tea is the kind of tea drunk in *chanoyu* or
the Japanese tea ceremony, a depiction of which in the
late-nineteenth-century woodblock print in plate 29
shows a group of elegantly dressed women about to
partake of thick tea. The woman making the tea is on the
point of ladling hot water from a cast-iron cauldron
sitting in a sunken hearth into a ceramic tea bowl in front
of her. To her left are a ceramic fresh-water jar, from
which water is taken to replenish the cauldron, a ceramic
tea caddy on which there rests a thin bamboo tea scoop,
and next to this a bamboo tea whisk. The textile bag to
her immediate left is for the tea caddy, and beside this,
just discernible beyond her lap, is a waste-water bowl.

These and other utensils can also be seen in plate 30,
which is of a print from the same series showing
preparations underway prior to the start of the tea

30. *Preparing for the tea ceremony, woodblock print, by Mizuno Toshikata, 1890–1900. V&A: E.3132–1905.*

ceremony. The woman on the left is placing a tea bowl she has removed from its storage box onto a shelf, next to a tea whisk. The woman on the right is using a mounted feather to dust off a lacquered tea caddy she has just filled with powdered tea ground in the stone mill to her right and then sieved in what looks like a two-tiered box in front of her. Lacquered tea caddies are used in the thin tea stage of the tea ceremony, when individual bowls of tea are made for each of the guests. This contrasts with the use of a ceramic tea caddy for the preceding thick tea stage, when a single bowlful of tea is ritualistically shared by all the guests.

The tea ceremony has its origins in the late fifteenth and sixteenth centuries, when successive tea masters, most famously Sen no Rikyū (1522–91), established the tenets that have underlain this distinctively Japanese cultural practice up to the present day. At its most profound, the tea ceremony is a quest for spiritual fulfilment through devotion to the making and serving of tea and, by extension, to the humble routine of daily life. This notion has its roots in the philosophy of Zen Buddhism. The tea ceremony has many styles and can be conducted in a variety of modes, ranging from the austere and subdued to the extravagant and flamboyant. This being said, the so-called '*wabi*' style of tea perfected by Rikyū lies at the heart of all forms of the tea ceremony. *Wabi* is a literary term suggestive of the idea of material deprivation. In the context of the tea ceremony it has come to mean the rejection of luxury and a taste for the simple, the understated and the incomplete.

The aestheticization of the spaces within which, and the utensils with which the tea ceremony is conducted has had a profound effect on

Japanese art and design, especially from the Momoyama period (1573–1615) onwards. The view in plate 32 is of a waiting arbour in the outer garden of a tea house complex whose oldest parts date from the beginning of the seventeenth century. The late-sixteenth- to early-seventeenth-century tea bowl and fresh-water jar in plate 31 and the slightly later tea caddy are good examples of Japanese ceramics made specifically for tea ceremony use. The vessels in plate 33 are examples of ceramics made for the so-called *kaiseki* meal. Having initially evolved in the sixteenth century as a corollary of the tea ceremony, of which indeed it still forms an integral part today, it was, more significantly, the starting point for the extreme sophistication of Japanese food culture that took place during the Edo period (1615–1868).

If whipped tea is nowadays primarily associated with the tea ceremony, the history of its use in Japan begins in the late twelfth century, when Zen Buddhist monks returning from China brought with them knowledge about Song dynasty (960–1279) methods of tea preparation. It was initially drunk mainly in temples, where, as well as being used as a digestive, it helped monks keep awake during their long hours of meditation. Rituals involving the ceremonial offering of tea to the founders of temples were also conducted. As time went by and the number of tea plantations increased, interest in tea drinking spread to other sections of society. Tea became known to ordinary people, to the extent that a typical feature of medieval life was the tea pedlar selling bowlfuls of tea by the roadside. Tea also came to play an important role in formal social interchange between members of the ruling military

32. *Tea garden with waiting arbour, Jo-an tea house complex, Inuyama. Author's photograph.*

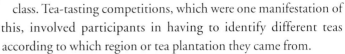

class. Tea-tasting competitions, which were one manifestation of this, involved participants in having to identify different teas according to which region or tea plantation they came from.

The custom of drinking steeped or infused tea is thought to have started in Japan in the late sixteenth century. Like boiled tea and whipped tea before it, this new form of tea drinking was introduced from China. While Kaempfer's comments suggest it was relatively well known about by the end of the seventeenth century, they also indicate that whipped tea continued to be consumed regularly by the powerful and wealthy. Steeped tea drinking did not come fully into its own until the eighteenth century, following the pioneering of a new method of tea leaf processing in the late 1730s. This involved steaming the leaves to stop fermentation rather than roasting them in the manner learnt from China. Tea produced in this way was fresher, greener and more flavoursome, and it was not long before steaming replaced the older roasting method in tea-growing areas throughout the country.

Historically the Japanese have used two methods to prepare steeped tea. The first, which died out during the early nineteenth century, involved putting tea leaves into a pot of boiling water and leaving the mixture to cool. Sometimes the brew was left to simmer, in which case the result was similar to that achieved through the *senjicha* method of boiling in a metal cauldron or kettle. The second method, which is the one familiar to us today, involved pouring boiling water over tea leaves placed in a teapot.[17]

Ceramic teapots were used for both of these ways of making tea. Those with overhead handles, like the example in Beato's photograph of a serving girl in plate 35, are known as

33. Shallow food dish, Oribe type stoneware, Mino kilns, early 17th century.
V&A: FE.73–1982.
Tall food container, Shino type stoneware, Mino kilns, end 16th–early 17th century.
V&A: 178A–1877.
Sake Bottle, Kiyomizu type stoneware, Kyoto kilns, 18th century.
V&A: C.1266–1917.

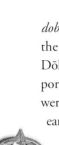

dobin. Those with side handles attached at right-angles to the spout, like the enamel-decorated example by the Kyoto-based potter Nin'ami Dōhachi (1783–1855) in plate 34, are known as *kyūsu.* Stoneware and porcelain teapots, which cracked if placed directly over a source of heat, were only used for the second way of making steeped tea. Heat-resistant earthenware teapots, on the other hand, could be used for either method of preparation. Earthenware teapots were also used simply to boil water, though this became less common as cast-iron kettles like the example in plate 36 gained popularity during the nineteenth century.

Dobin are generally larger than *kyūsu*, which are often small enough to fit into the palm of the hand. Differences in sizes of teapots and variations in ways of infusing the tea leaves relate to the quality of tea used. Japanese leaf tea comes in three main grades. The lowest grade, *bancha*, is made from leaves picked late in the growing season. *Sencha* is made from younger, more tender leaves harvested in spring. The exceptional flavour of *gyokuro* (literally 'jade dew'), the highest quality grade, results from the tea bushes being shaded from the sun during part of the growing season. Tea plantations with the facility to produce *gyokuro* were first established in the 1830s and 1840s. *Bancha* requires the water to be as hot as possible and in the past would also have been the variety of tea used for extended boiling. *Sencha* and *gyokuro*, which are usually prepared in *kyūsu* rather than *dobin*, are steeped in water that has been boiled and left for a short period to cool.

The term *sencha* also gives its name to *senchadō*, literally the 'Way of Steeped Tea'. This was a formalization of steeped tea drinking practices that had parallels with, but was developed as a conscious alternative to, the tea ceremony.[18] It initially flourished in Kyoto and Osaka among late-eighteenth-century intellectuals with an interest in Chinese literati culture, and became widespread during the nineteenth century. As with the tea ceremony, it gave rise to a demand for new types of utensils, the majority of which, like the Dōhachi teapot and other items in plate 34, were in distinctly Chinese styles.

Today, at the start of the twenty-first century, the Japanese love of tea, coupled with an increasing awareness of its medicinal benefits, is as strong as it has ever been. Japan ranks among the world's top five consumers and top ten producers of tea, and boasts an industry that is one of the most technologically advanced of its kind. Green tea, which has always been the principal kind of tea produced in Japan, is drunk the most frequently, but imported black tea is widely available and oolong tea is also highly popular. In the West we continue to steep our tea largely in the manner learnt from the Chinese four hundred years ago. The Japanese, on the other hand, consume both steeped tea and powdered

37. Fresh-water jar, Shino type stoneware, by Suzuki Osamu, 1989.
V&A: FE.29–1989.
Tea bowl, Black Raku type high-fired earthenware, by Raku Kichizaemon XV, 1992.
V&A: FE.535–1992.
Tea caddy, lacquer on bamboo core, by Ikeda Iwao, 1988.
V&A: FE.29–2001.

38. *Tea set, porcelain, by Yoshikawa Masamichi, 1994. V&A: FE.15–1995.*

tea, though much less of the latter (if one discounts its use in the making of green tea ice cream) than in former times. The kind of boiled *senjicha* described by Kaempfer as being the preserve of 'vulgar and Country people' is no longer found. In its place, however, there is a bewildering variety of pre-prepared tea-based beverages dispensed in cans and bottles by Japan's ubiquitous automatic vending machines.

At the other extreme, which sees consumers indulging their passion for the exotic, there is a thriving market not only for expensive European brands of tea, but also, more recently, for rare single-estate teas from Taiwan and India, particularly Darjeeling. There is also much interest in *gongfucha*, a Chinese form of steeped tea preparation that involves the placing of the teapot in a basin of hot water prior to the pouring onto the tea leaves of hot or boiling water. Quality does not necessarily preclude convenience, however, and for those disinterested in or too busy to be bothered with elaborate methods of preparation, it is now possible to find even the finest varieties of leaf tea in tea-bag form. What is more, the self-fill sachets sold in Japanese supermarkets allow consumers to make their own tea bags and give them unlimited choice in the kinds of tea they can prepare by this increasingly prevalent method.

The continuing centrality of tea drinking in modern Japanese life, both in its ritualistic and everyday forms, is accompanied, as in the past, by a thriving culture of tea utensil production. This includes everything from cheap, commercial manufactures to one-off studio works produced, like the examples in plates 37 and 38, by leading contemporary makers. While hard, reusable plastic cups are increasingly common in mass catering establishments, disposable cups are generally less prevalent, for tea drinking at least, than in Europe and North America. Even in the quick turnaround, throwaway culture of modern Japan, the preference is for tea unadulterated by the taste of waterproofed paper or polystyrene.

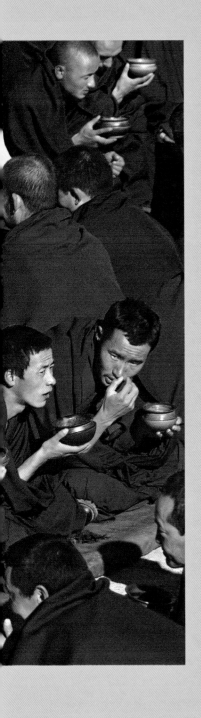

4

TIBET AND THE HIMALAYAS

JOHN CLARKE

'Any good Tibetan drinks fifty to sixty
cups of tea every day of his life.'
FREDERICK SPENCER CHAPMAN, 1907–71

Tibet and the Himalayas

THE FIRST RECORD OF TEA BEING IMPORTED into Tibet is found in Chinese annals of the Tang dynasty corresponding to the reign of the second great king of Tibet, Trisong Detsen (742–97).[19] From the late eleventh to early fifteenth century tea was bartered by the Chinese government in Sichuan Province for fine Tibetan war horses.[20] Despite the imposition of the death penalty on smugglers, there was also a huge black market in contraband tea. Although tea came to be drunk throughout Tibet, the Tibetans modified what they borrowed, as with other key imports from China, transforming it into something distinctively their own. While the Chinese have historically preferred green tea, brick tea made from fermented black leaves has been the norm in most parts of Tibet. This can be explained in terms of the lengthiness of the journey from China into Tibet and the ability of brick tea sewn into yak skins to withstand knocks, rain and other conditions unfavourable to the transport of loose-leaf tea.

With the establishment of the north Indian tea industry in the mid-nineteenth century, the monopoly enjoyed by Chinese tea was challenged for the first time. British traders hoped to use the trading agencies[21] set up as a result of the British military expedition of 1904[22] to capitalize on the enormous Tibetan market for tea. Their optimism proved misplaced, however, for the Tibetans never found Indian tea to their taste, even though it was much cheaper than Chinese tea. Even the Ladakhis, who lived furthest from China in the far west of the Tibetan cultural area, continued to insist on drinking Chinese tea, declaring that the tea sold by the British was 'a poison capable of giving the consumer every sort of disease'.[23]

Almost all the tea imported into Tibet was grown in Yazhou, an area in Sichuan Province about 100 kilometres from the Tibetan border.[24] Except for a small amount of loose-leaf tea traded via Songpan to the nomads of north-east Tibet, the majority travelled in brick form through the border town of Kangding, a major clearing-house for tea since at least

the early fifteenth century. Prior to being sent to Kangding, the tea was compacted either by steaming and pressing into tubes of bamboo matting, or by soaking in boiled tea and moulding into rectangular bricks called *dum* or *barka*. Once they were dry, the tea bricks were placed in wickerwork tubes to be carried by porters (plate 40) through country so rugged and mountainous that it was impassable for pack animals.

In Kangding, a bustling town of mixed population, Tibetan merchants bought tea from Chinese vendors, duty having to be paid both on entry and departure. From Kangding the tea was transported into Tibet by yak caravan. For this part of the journey bundles of twelve bricks were wrapped together in tightly stretched wet hide. As the hide dried, each bale became hard and virtually unbreakable. Two bales, each weighing about sixty pounds (27 kg), formed one yak load, and one caravan often comprised hundreds of yaks. At the start of the twentieth century Tibet's annual consumption of tea varied from ten to nearly fourteen million pounds (4,500–6,400 tonnes). This means that the number of yak-loads of tea leaving Kangding was between 80,000 and 120,000 per year or, on average, in the order of 200 to 300 each day.

The 1,500-kilometre journey to Lhasa was a slow and often hazardous one. Yak caravans usually took a year to reach their destination and the animals had to be changed regularly along the way. Armed retainers were employed to fight off brigands, who were a particular problem in the nomad country of north-east Tibet.

Although the trade was theoretically open to all, in reality it was largely dominated by government officials. The largest traders were the Dalai Lama and Panchen Lama, the two most powerful figures in the Tibetan political hierarchy. These and other dignitaries regularly sent their agents to the eastern frontier to arrange the purchase and shipment of tea.

By scrutinizing, chewing or burning a few leaves, Tibetans could distinguish different types, vintages and grades of tea. Five main grades were available in Tibet. The two best grades, which were largely pure tea, were drunk by the nobility and prosperous merchants. Most people drank the third and fourth grades, which were mixtures of tea and chopped twigs of bushes and small trees. The lowest grade, called *shingka* or 'wood tea' due to its consisting largely if not wholly of chopped twigs, was drunk by the poor. Among the largest consumers of tea were the three government monasteries situated close to Lhasa, which between them housed close to twenty thousand monks. Before the fall of the Qing dynasty in 1911 they received a yearly subsidy from the Chinese emperor of eight million pounds (3,600 tonnes) of tea. This was in addition to the annual supply they were entitled to from the Lhasa government.

Brick tea was, and is, consumed throughout the Tibetan world, including outlying areas such as the former kingdoms of Sikkim and Ladakh, both now part of northern India, and the present kingdom of Bhutan. It was also exported from China via north-east Tibet by horse or camel caravan into Mongolia, where Tibetan religious and cultural practices prevailed.

The universality of brick tea in the Tibetan world led to its use as a form of currency. Tea could be bartered against practically anything, and workmen and servants were routinely paid in it. In 1891 the American ethnographer William Rockhill followed local custom by paying nomads in north-east Tibet a small brick of tea for a sheep and a piece of cloth.[25]

Visitors to Tibet are wont to focus on the unique and colourful process of making 'butter tea'.[26] Quintessentially Tibetan though this is, it is by

41. *Tea drinking during a picnic party in a park outside Lhasa, by Sir Charles Bell, 1921. Courtesy of the British Library.*

no means the only way tea has been, or is, prepared in Tibet. In the eastern province of Kham, for example, tea is either consumed black, or salt and milk are added to make *O cha* or milk tea. In Amdo, north-east Tibet, and in Mongolia, unsalted milk tea is common. In the nomad areas of Amdo one also finds black tea served with a knob of butter placed on the cup's rim. Butter tea in its characteristic form is found principally in central and southern Tibet.

To make butter tea a tea brick is crushed or pounded into powder and put into a pan of cold water. This is heated and boiled for about five minutes, a small amount of soda, obtained from the shores of the lakes on the northern Tibetan plateau, being added to give a reddish tinge and to draw out the flavour. After boiling, the tea is poured through a strainer, traditionally made of brass or horsehair but sometimes today made of plastic, into a long cylindrical wooden container known as a *cha dong* (plates 42, 43). Butter and salt are added and the mixture is vigorously churned with a long plunger until it is thoroughly emulsified. Repetitive work of this kind is often accompanied by song in Tibet. The tea song, though no longer much used today, is a delightful celebration of the origins and coming together of the drink's ingredients. The words were sung while churning the mixture:

42. *Boy monk at Samye Monastery, southern Tibet, making butter tea in a tea churn, by Norma Joseph, about 1985. Courtesy of the Royal Geographical Society, London.*

> 'From the Chinese country comes the tea flower beautiful.
> From the northern plain comes the small white salt.
> From the Tibetan country comes the yak butter like gold.
> The birthplace and dwelling place are not the same –
> But they all meet together in the little belted churn.' [27]

The resulting yellowish beverage compares more to a clear soup than to the European idea of tea. It is a very effective means of replacing the fat and salt lost by the body in high-altitude regions like Tibet. Westerners have tended to find butter tea unpalatable because of the use of rancid

43. *Tea churn, wood and brass, Ladakh, about 1975.*
V&A: IS 4–2000.
Tea brick, Ladakh, about 1999.
V&A: IS 5–2000.
Teapot, wood with brass plaques, Tibet, 18th century.
V&A: IS 22–1965.
Teapot, earthenware inset with fragments of Chinese porcelain, eastern Tibet, about 1900.
V&A: IM 29–1910.

butter. Heinrich Harrer, who lived in Lhasa for seven years during the 1940s, related how he 'never got used to the green or yellowish surface film on the tea' and 'found the smell nearly nauseating'. But he learnt to 'blow back the floating fat' so that he 'could drink only the tea underneath'.[28] Harrer explained the rancidness of the butter as resulting from the way in which the milk from the *dri* or female yak was obtained in only small daily amounts, which meant that it could take weeks or months to fill the yak skin bags in which it was stored. If butter tea is made with fresh butter, the taste is quite different and altogether more pleasant.

Tea is still taken by everyone in Tibet, monks included (plate 39), and few activities proceed without it. Daily consumption can be forty cups or more, etiquette dictating that the cup of a guest should never be allowed to become empty. Placing one's hand over the cup is the usual way to prevent it being refilled.

Because metal teapots impart a bitter flavour to tea and do not stay hot for long, they have never been used on a daily basis. Until the advent of thermoses, which are now universal in the Tibetan world, tea for everyday consumption was kept in earthenware vessels (plate 43) placed on stoves or braziers filled with smouldering yak dung. More robust wooden teapots (plate 43) were also used, especially by the nomads of north and north-east Tibet. Families who could afford them, however, also owned copper, brass or silver teapots decorated with auspicious emblems, lotus flowers

44. *Dragon-handled teapot, silver-gilt, silver and brass-gilt, inset with turquoises, Hemis Monastery, Ladakh, 19th century. V&A: IM 112–1927. Tea bowl, lathe-turned willow or poplar burl with silver lining and silver-gilt central boss, Ladakh, about 1850. V&A: 1432–1883.*

and scrollwork (plate 44). These were used on special occasions such as marriages, festivals and visits by important guests. When not in use they were displayed prominently on kitchen shelves, and were handed down through the generations as family heirlooms. Metalwork teapots were made in various shapes, the most common sort being the round-bodied teapot decorated with lotus petals, symbols of both water and spiritual purity. The most elaborate varieties, which have been used since at least the seventeenth century, are embellished with dragon-shaped handles. Their spouts emerge from the gaping jaws of *makara*, mythical aquatic monsters of Indian origin, and their bodies are ornamented with pierced-work plaques bearing birds, animals and auspicious Buddhist emblems. These teapots were used not only in Tibet but also in Ladakh, Bhutan and Mongolia, with only small variations in workmanship and shape indicating their different geographical origins.[29] Although finely decorated teapots are made less often today than they used to be, their owners continue to use them on special occasions.

In the past every Tibetan owned a *por pa* or tea bowl (plate 44).[30] These were used both for drinking tea and for food. When not in use they were wiped or licked clean and kept in the large pocket of the *chupa,* the standard garment worn by both men and women. *Por pa* were carried about the person and brought out whenever required. The most highly prized examples were lathe-turned from knotted burl wood, a whole burl being required to produce a single bowl. Beech, box, chestnut, maple and silver birch were the main varieties of timber used. Wood with convoluted knotting was valued not only for its beauty when polished, but because it was particularly resistant to hot liquids. The best cups were also believed to split on contact with poison. Their rich light brown colour was often complemented by the addition of an inner lining of sheet silver. The bulbous knots were called *ba,* the Tibetan term for goitre, or *dza*. These were believed to emit a glow that could lead one to them at night, deep in the recesses of the forest. *Dza* gave its name to Dzayul,

45. *Cup stand and cover, silver and silver-gilt, workshop of Khem Raj Sakya, Patan, Nepal, 1982. V&A: IS 16–1989. Cup, porcelain, Chinese, possibly 18th century. V&A: 410–1906.*

literally 'the country of the *dza*', the area in south-east Tibet where some of the finest bowls were made. Bowls were also made in the forested areas of Kongpo and Dagpo in eastern central Tibet, and in China, in the border provinces of Yunnan and Gansu, from where they were imported.

Wealthier Tibetan families also possessed elaborate silver or brass cup stands (plate 45) for use with jade or porcelain cups. They were fitted with metal covers to keep the tea from cooling. Highly prized Khotanese jade cups and expensive porcelain cups were protected during travelling by being packed into purpose made iron cases (plate 46). Cups and stands of this quality were only used by household heads or important guests.

As suggested earlier, monasteries have been among the largest consumers of tea in Tibet. Even today, tea is served to monks gathered in their hundreds for large religious services. Between periods of chanting or the recitation of texts, monk attendants serve their colleagues by pouring tea from large brass or copper jugs (plate 47) into individual tea bowls placed on low tables in front of them. When laymen sponsor the reading of sacred scriptures, they also pay for tea for the participating monks. This can involve considerable expense. The cost of tea for a three-week reading of texts at the Lhasa New Year festival in 1891 cost the equivalent at the time of $100,000.[31]

At the large monasteries of central Tibet tea has traditionally been brewed in enormous cast copper or bronze cauldrons almost a metre deep and not much less than two metres in diameter (plate 48). These are heated by fires from below. The same method is still used today, although older cauldrons in some kitchens have been replaced by modern aluminium vessels. Monk servers fill their teapots by dipping them into the cauldrons and carry them into the prayer halls on their shoulders. The teapots have two handles to permit steadier pouring (plate 49). An ordinary monk's wooden tea bowl is similar in shape and size to a layman's but distinguishable by an extra ridge on its shoulder (plate 49). Important religious figures use porcelain or jade cups placed on embossed silver stands similar to those used by wealthy laymen.

The age-old rituals of tea making also continue to be practised by the majority of ordinary people in Tibet, Bhutan and Ladakh. Tea is still boiled, churned and served in traditional wooden cups or in more modern ceramic or glass containers. When available, Tibetan refugees in India make use of imported wooden cups made in north-west Nepal. The introduction of the thermos has, however, resulted in the virtual disappearance of the brazier and teapot as a means of keeping tea hot. Tibetans in exile consume much less butter tea than they did in Tibet and have largely switched to *chai*, Indian tea made by boiling together tea, milk and water, sometimes with the addition of sugar. This is especially true of the younger generation, though they too may partake of butter tea on festive occasions such as New Year.

48. *Monk tea servers gathered around a tea cauldron at Gyantse, southern Tibet, possibly by Henry Martin, 1911. V&A Picture Library: BW66217.000.*

49. *Monastic teapot, copper and brass, Ganden Monastery, central Tibet, late 19th century, acquired during the 1904 British expedition to Tibet. V&A: 456–1905. Monk's tea bowl, lathe-turned wood burl, Ladakh, 19th century. Private collection.*

RUSSIA,
IRAN AND
TURKEY

JENNIFER SCARCE

'Ecstasy is a glass full of tea and a piece
of sugar in the mouth.'
ALEKSANDR PUSHKIN, 1797–1837

Russia, Iran and Turkey

THE DRINKING OF *chai* IN RUSSIA, *chay* in Iran and *çay* in Turkey is one of the more lasting results of centuries of political, economic and social interaction between these three major cultures. With the frequent encroachment of one power upon the other, their common boundaries have been subject to regular negotiation throughout history. The arrival of the Mongols ushered in a period of temporary unification. Genghis Khan and his descendants dominated Russia from the mid-thirteenth to late fifteenth century, until challenged by the principality of Moscow. Iran was subject to Mongol control between the mid-twelfth and mid-fourteenth centuries. Mongol power also extended briefly into eastern Turkey following Tamerlane's defeat of the Ottoman sultan Beyazit I at the battle of Ankara in 1402.

The relations maintained between the three cultures long after the waning of Mongol power resulted in a complex pattern of mutual influence in the realms of language, social customs, dress, food and drink. Wealthy Russians, for example, benefited from the rich culinary traditions of Iran and Turkey, which in turn depended on the importation of spices such as ginger, cardamom and cinnamon from Asia. The drinks served with or separately from meals in Russia, Turkey and Iran were of various kinds. Christian communities drank alcohol in the form of beer, wine and spirits, whereas Muslim communities drank non-alcoholic beverages prepared from water, yoghurt and different kinds of fruit juice. Hot beverages included both coffee and tea. Coffee, which originated in Yemen, was known in Turkey and Iran by the sixteenth century, and was introduced into Russia at the time of Peter the Great (r.1682–1725). Tea, which has now replaced coffee in Russia and the Middle East as the most widely consumed form of hot drink, did not become universally popular until the nineteenth century.

Tea is said to have been introduced into Russia in 1616 when a Cossack by the name of Tyumenets returned from a diplomatic mission to Mongolia with samples of Chinese tea. Two years later, in 1618, a gift of

(Previous pages)
50. *Detail from plate 57.*

several chests of tea were brought by a Chinese embassy to the Russian court in Moscow. Then, in 1638, a further gift of two hundred packets of tea were sent as a gift by the Mongol ruler to Tsar Mikhail Fedorovich (r.1613–45), who was apparently not at all impressed and made it clear that he would have preferred sables.[32] Russia's subsequent growth into a major tea drinking nation owed much to the opening of the overland caravan route across Mongolia following the signing of the Nerchinsk treaty with China in 1689.[33] The amount of tea imported into Russia gradually increased during the eighteenth century, towards the end of which, during the period of adulation of European social customs at the court of Catherine the Great (r.1763–96), tea drinking became fashionable among the Russian nobility. Catherine, it is recorded, 'dines at two, withdraws to her apartments soon after dinner' and 'drinks tea at five'.[34]

Although a certain amount was also imported via Europe, the majority of tea drunk in Russia, nearly all of it black, travelled from China by camel caravan. Until the 1850s this took the form of loose-leaf tea packed into chests. From the 1860s this was supplemented and indeed overtaken by brick tea made at Russian factories established in Hankou, a major tea trading centre on the banks of the Yangtze River in Hubei Province, and elsewhere. The subsequent building of the Trans-Siberian Railway, which was completed at the start of the twentieth century, brought a close to the era of the camel caravan. Tea was either shipped to Vladivostok and then transported across Russia by rail, or it was shipped all the way to the Black Sea port of Odessa. The early twentieth century also saw the establishment of domestic tea plantations in Georgia, at the eastern end of the Black Sea. The much greater availability of tea resulting from these developments went hand in hand with the spread of tea drinking to all sectors of Russian society.

The defining feature of Russian tea culture has long been the samovar (plate 51), a simple but highly effective piece of equipment that provides a constant supply of tea. The samovar, literally 'self-boiler', is lovingly featured in Russian literature and frequently appears in paintings and photographs (plates 52, 53, 55). It consists of a metal urn which is filled with water and heated by pine cones or charcoal fired through a central funnel. A strong brew of tea is made in a teapot, which is kept warm by being placed on top of the samovar. The tea is poured into a teacup or tea glass and then diluted as required with hot water added from the tap at the base of the urn. Samovars were not produced in large numbers until the late eighteenth century. The majority were made in Tula, a long-established metalworking centre south of Moscow, where Ivan Lisitsyn opened a specialist samovar workshop in 1778.[35] Most samovars, like the one illustrated here, were made of brass, but more luxurious examples executed in gold and silver were fashionable and presented on occasion

52. *Woodcutters taking a break for tea and bread, Ukraine, by Florence Farmborough, 1908–1909. Reproduced from J. Jolliffe (ed.),* Florence Farmborough, Russian Album, *1908–1918, 1979.*

53. Marchande Buvant du Thé, *oil on canvas, by Boris Koustodiev, 1918. Russian Museum, St Petersburg. Reproduced from N. Novoouspenski,* Le Musée Russe Peinture, *1974.*

as gifts to the imperial court.[36]

While the samovar was a purely Russian invention, the other objects used for serving and drinking tea were either European or made in European style. The Imperial Russian Porcelain Factory founded in 1744 under the patronage of Empress Elizabeth Petrovna (r.1741–62) responded to the fashion for tea by producing elegant services of matching teapots, jugs, sugar bowls, cups, saucers and trays decorated in strong colours and vivid designs. The fine examples from the early nineteenth century in plate 54 have enamel-decorated panels of baskets of roses reserved against a lavish ground of dark blue and gold. Tea was drunk not only from porcelain cups but also from glasses set in elaborately crafted metal holders. This custom, which began in the nineteenth century, is still practised in Russia today.

The advent of the samovar and the start of domestic manufacture of tea wares are indicative of the growing popularity of tea drinking from the

54. *Tea service, porcelain, St Petersburg, early 19th century. V&A: C.47–52–1933.*

the eighteenth century onwards. At home, the aristocracy drank tea continually between and after meals. Tea was also served at public performances and on celebratory occasions. The ballerina Tamara Karsavina, writing about a matinée performance by students of the Mariinsky Company in December 1896, noted the welcome provision of tea on a cold St Petersburg day: 'Huge samovars steamed outside the stage door. …In the interval tea and refreshments were served in several foyers and the waiting staff wore their gala red livery with the Imperial eagles.'[37]

Tea was served more formally in the social ritual of afternoon tea, a European custom followed by the upper and aspirant middle classes. Plate 53 shows a well-dressed merchant's wife seated at a balcony enjoying a lavish repast set out on embroidered cloths and napkins. The watermelon and grapes would have been imported from Georgia. In the basket is an assortment of sweet poppyseed rolls and a portion of *kulich*, a type of yeast cake filled with dried fruit and almonds. All this and the

55. *Tea and cherries at a dacha near Moscow, by Florence Farmborough, 1910. Reproduced from J.Jolliffe (ed.),* Florence Farmborough, Russian Album, 1908–1918, *1979.*

gleaming samovar and richly decorated porcelain tea service are testimony to the hostess's considerable affluence. She has poured her tea into a saucer to cool it before sipping it without milk in the Russian manner. Sweeteners were not added to tea but taken separately. This could be in the form of lumps of sugar or, as here, jam served in a covered glass bowl. In summer orange, lemon or cherry juice was sometimes mixed with tea to make a cooling refreshment. In plate 55, which shows an upper class family at their dacha outside Moscow, the tea is more modestly accompanied by cherries and plain cake. At the lower end of the social spectrum, plate 52 shows a group of woodmen breaking for tea and a slice of rye bread. The brass samovar, very similar to that illustrated in plate 51, is much plainer than those in plates 53 and 55.

'Tea is the national drink of Persia, owing to centuries of intercourse with China, and the tea shop is the club of the middle and lower class Persian, where he can talk to his friends or listen to the song of the caged bulbul.' [38]

Although correct in stating the centrality of tea drinking in Iran, Ella Sykes, who kept house for her brother Percy, British Consul to Kerman and Baluchistan, between 1895 and 1897, would probably not have known that the custom was relatively recent. References to tea drinking before the nineteenth century are few. Two early German travellers to Iran briefly refer to the practice; Adam Olearius in the 1630s observed that the Iranians liked to drink green China tea sweetened with sugar[39] and Engelbert Kaempfer in 1683 noted that he was served tea in Shemakli and Qazvin,[40] towns in the north of the country subject to Russian cultural influence.

During the early nineteenth century tea was still an expensive commodity enjoyed only by the upper classes. It was used to entertain special guests such as the French envoy, Pierre Amédée Jaubert, who in

1806 was offered both tea and coffee in Qazvin by Fath Ali Shah (r.1797–1834).[41] Changing political circumstances such as the Russian conquest of the northern province of Azerbaijan in 1828 and Britain's growing strategic and commercial interest in Iran gave rise to economic conditions conducive to the spread of tea drinking. Russia was keen to export sugar to Iran, for example, while the British sought new markets for the tea grown in their plantations in northern India. This was followed by the emergence of local industries to produce tea and sugar. Mirza Taqi Khan, the Amir-e Kabir or Prime Minister of Iran from 1848 to 1851, established factories in Mazandaran to refine locally grown sugar cane into both granulated and lump sugar. Tentative efforts to grow tea from the 1870s onwards eventually bore fruit when Kasef al-Saltana, the Iranian Consul to India, succeeded in cultivating Assamese tea in the Caspian province of Gilan. This was in 1902. From these modest beginnings, the Iranian tea industry has grown to such an extent that the country now produces more than half of what it consumes by way of this important commodity.

Since the 1850s infused black tea taken without milk has been Iran's most popular drink. It was and continues to be consumed during and between meals, at formal and informal receptions, wedding parties, New Year celebrations, and in bazaars, offices and shops. Following the introduction of the samovar in the nineteenth century, tea in Iran has been made in the Russian manner. The Amir-e Kabir, Mirza Taqi Khan, after receiving two silver samovars with matching services in 1850, one from a Russian merchant and the other from the French government, was encouraged to subsidize a master craftsman in Isfahan to start local production of samovars. Samovars of beaten, hammered and polished brass in the traditional style continue to be made in centres such as Borujerd in Luristan province and are sold in the bazaars of all cities.[42] The example in plate 56 is rather different, being a very tinny mass-produced version with an electric element, albeit in traditional shape. Russia's influence on Iranian tea culture has also been felt in the realm of ceramics. From the 1880s until about 1915, the Gardner and Kuznetsov porcelain factories developed lines of porcelain teapots and tea bowls decorated in bright colours and floral motifs specifically for the Iranian market. These and ceramics imported from Europe were a more expensive and prestigious alternative to the small glasses that continue to be used on a day-to-day basis.

The large-scale oil paintings that are among the most distinctive artistic products of nineteenth-century Iran are invaluable sources of information about the social customs of their time. Isma'il Jalayir's charming depiction of a group of harem ladies making music and taking tea is full of fascinating detail (plates 50, 57). The women stand and sit on a verandah overlooking a garden. Spread informally on the ground in front of them is a selection of fresh fruit, including figs, pomegranates and a watermelon, together with the various pieces of equipment needed to make and serve tea. The plain teapot on top of the brass samovar and the decorated cups and saucers on the round tray are made of porcelain, probably imported from Russia or Europe. The women would have had a choice of ways of sweetening their tea. Sugar, except among Europeanized Iranians, was usually offered separately in chunks, either to be nibbled as sweets or to be held between the teeth as the tea was sipped. Nuts coated with sugar and dried fruits were also served, as were honey and cherry jam. The bowl on the left of the tray is piled high with what appear to be either sugar lumps or sugared sweets. The atmosphere of Isma'il Jalayir's tea party is echoed in an entry of 12 January 1850 in the diary of Lady Sheil, wife of the British representative to Tehran, concerning an invitation to tea with the mother of Nasiruddin Shah (r.1848–96): 'Tea, coffee and pipes were brought in repeatedly, and after some time a nice collation of fruit, various kinds of sherbets, ices and cakes were spread on the table and on the ground.'[43]

The introduction of tea to Turkey, where, contrary to the popular perception of Turkey as a coffee-drinking country, tea is now consumed in such large quantities that it qualifies for the status of national drink, occurred much later than in Russia or Iran. The Ottoman traveller Evliya Celebi (1610–83) noted that the ruler of Bitlis in eastern Turkey enjoyed both fruit sherbets and tea[44], but the only other historical references that survive concern tea parties among the European diplomatic community in nineteenth-century Istanbul. The dramatic switch from coffee to tea that took place in the early twentieth century was the outcome of a political decision rather than the result of gradual economic and social change. Tea growing, a few unsuccessful attempts at which had been made during the last years of the Ottoman Turkish Empire, was taken up after the Ataturk Revolution of 1925 as one of the many state enterprises on which the new domestic economy was to be built. The humid Black Sea region was found to be suitable for the growing of tea, whose consumption the government encouraged as a replacement for costly imported coffee. The relative cheapness of tea and the ease with which it could be prepared recommended it to a government both practically and ideologically in search of a beverage that could be enjoyed by all members of Turkish society. Turkey's tea industry was established in the 1920s with seeds imported from neighbouring Georgia. Centred on the town of Rize, it is still dominated by the State Tea Corporation, one of Turkey's largest enterprises.

Turkish tea is infused and diluted to taste as in Russia and Iran. It is usually served with cakes and biscuits and is always accompanied by sugar. Rather than using a samovar, however, the teapot is kept warm by being placed on the top of a large kettle of hot water. The tea is poured into a glass and diluted to taste by adding water from the kettle. Nowadays the principles of this somewhat improvised system have been incorporated into sleek automatic electric kettles with integral teapots that sit on top of them (plate 58).

Plate 59 is a magazine illustration from the 1920s showing a group of Turkish women taking tea. Seated in egalitarian fashion around a table in a public tea garden, they symbolize the new Turkish woman of the Republican era. Their faces are completely uncovered and their fashionably bobbed hair is visible below their tightly knotted head-scarves. In keeping with their clothing, which is unmistakably European in style, they drink their tea from a European tea service consisting of a

58. *Electric kettle with integral teapot, made by Arcelik, Turkey, 1999. Courtesy of Mr Edwin Davies and the Strix Group Ltd.*

59. *Turkish women taking tea, about 1920–30. Reproduced from P. Tuglaci,* Women of Istanbul in Ottoman Times, *1984.*

60. *Tea glass, saucer and spoon, Turkey, about 1994. Courtesy of the author.*

teapot, a sugar bowl and a milk jug as well as cups and saucers. These would have been modish alternatives to traditional tea glasses set in elaborate filigree holders (plate 61). In contemporary Turkey both cups and glasses are used in the home and in restaurants and cafés.

Tulip-shaped glasses with matching saucers and spoons are a common and widely distributed product of Turkey's leading glassware factories (plate 60).

At the beginning of the new millennium, tea drinking continues to flourish in Russia, Iran and Turkey. New varieties of tea are grown, imported and blended. The ubiquitous tea bag has made its appearance as elsewhere, but, as has been seen, the samovar and its Turkish counterpart have survived through the clever marrying of modern technology with traditional functionality.

61. *Left: Glass or cup holder, silver filigree, Iran, 19th century. V&A: M.120–1909.*

Right: Glass or cup holder, silver-gilt filigree with enamels, Turkey, 19th century. V&A: 786–1891.

6

WESTERN EUROPE

HILARY YOUNG

'Tea's proper use is to amuse the idle, and relax the
studious, and dilute the full meals of those who cannot
use exercise, and will not use abstinence.'
SAMUEL JOHNSON, 1709–64

Western Europe

(Previous pages)
62. See plate 66.

T EA FIRST REACHED EUROPE DURING the first half of the seventeenth
century, when, as an exotic imported luxury, it began to enjoy a
restricted market in England, France and the Netherlands.[45] The
eighteenth century saw the enthusiastic adoption of the drink by the
British and Dutch, and it was during these years that tea became firmly
established as the national drink of Great Britain. Although German and
French consumption of tea increased during the latter part of the
nineteenth century, coffee remained by far the more popular drink; and
there are still many European coffee-drinking countries, particularly in
the south, that have never taken to tea at all.

Europeans first heard about tea from travellers to East Asia during the
sixteenth century. According to the account of a Persian traveller
published in Venice in 1559, tea should be drunk 'as hot as you can bear
it', an idea that would have seemed strange to Europeans, who rarely
consumed food or drink very hot at that time.[46] Significantly, the traveller
went on state that tea was an antidote to fever, headache, stomach-ache
and other pains, for it was as a costly medicinal herb that tea was first
taken up in the West. There are several exaggerated accounts of tea's
medicinal qualities dating from the mid-seventeenth century, one of the
best known being an advertisement of about 1660 for Thomas Garway's
London coffee-shop.[47] At this time most tea drunk in Europe was
imported by the Dutch. Writing in 1653, a Jesuit missionary returning
from the East noted that 'the Dutch bring tea from China to Paris',
adding that it 'must be regarded as a precious medicament'.[48] The Dutch
East India Company had first imported tea in 1610 and made it an article
of regular commerce in 1637. The word 'tea' – adopted, with variations,
by many western languages – comes from the Fujian term used by
Chinese merchants in Bantam, where the Dutch had established a
trading station. Had they traded elsewhere, we may well have adopted
the Cantonese or Mandarin word *cha*, as indeed did the Portuguese, who
probably first encountered the drink in the region of Canton

63. A Family Taking
Tea, *oil on canvas,
attributed to Richard
Collins, about 1727.
V&A: P.9–1934.*

(Guangzhou). The Dutch dominated the European trade in tea until 1678, when the English first imported it on a commercial scale.

By the time the English East India Company began trading in tea, the drink was well established at the English court, where it was no longer valued primarily for its medicinal benefits, but was drunk socially, as an invigorating beverage – a significant shift in emphasis. In 1660 Charles II had returned from exile among the tea-drinking Dutch, and two years later married Catherine of Braganza from Portugal. The Portuguese had been the first Europeans to encounter tea, having controlled the trade routes with East Asia until about 1600, and by the mid-seventeenth century were already drinking it at court. According to tradition, the new queen's passion for tea did much to popularize the drink in England, although recent research indicates that there may be little evidence for this.[49]

We should not lose sight here of the extraordinarily high price of tea in this early period. In the years around 1660 Thomas Garway's London shop was selling tea for between 16 and 60 shillings a pound (80p to £3 for 0.45 kg); and in 1664 a little over two pounds of tea, costing £4 5s 0d (£4.25), was considered a suitable gift for the king.[50] By the first decade of the eighteenth century, when the fashion for tea was rapidly gaining ground, the price for standard grade tea had dropped to about 12–14 shillings (60–70p) a pound, a sum roughly equal to the weekly wage of a master craftsman at that time.[51] Clearly, at such prices the drink was confined to the rich. That being so, its consumption became something to show off about; and so the tea ceremony came into being, allowing the host to make an elaborate display of wealth, worldly know-how and command of etiquette, at the same time as extending hospitality to guests. The expense of doing so could be considerable: according to a London magazine of 1744 it could cost more

64. *Teapot, silver-gilt, London, about 1685. V&A: M.48–1939.*

65. *Tea bowl and saucer, enamelled copper mounted in silver-gilt, mark of Elias Adam, Augsburg, about 1720. V&A: 1937–1898.*

to maintain a fashionable tea table, with its expensive tea and utensils, than to keep two children and a nurse.[52]

Despite its expense, tea came to play an essential role in the social life of both the British and the Dutch. Unlike food, it could be offered to anyone at any time without inconvenience and without breaking any of the rules of decorum. Its service provided a focal point for social activities, enabling people of differing rank to meet and converse, and helping to spread the 'polite' values of refinement, gentility and sociability.

In early eighteenth-century Britain and Holland tea was usually prepared by the lady of the house in front of her guests. It was habitually taken in the mid-afternoon, after dinner, but as the century progressed it was also more often drunk at breakfast. English and Dutch satires of this date frequently associate tea drinking with women – as in *'Tea Smitten Ladies'*, a Dutch play of 1701, and in satires by Alexander Pope, Colley Cibber and Jonathan Swift. Dining etiquette lent force to this association in eighteenth-century Britain, where women were required to withdraw and take tea after dinner, leaving their menfolk at the table to linger over wine; only after having exhausted the possibilities of wine and conversation would men join women in drinking tea. Early English and Dutch paintings of tea drinking emphasize the role of women, who are frequently shown taking all the social initiative, with the men taking their cues from them (plates 62, 63, 66).

66. Two Ladies and A Gentleman Drinking Tea, *oil on canvas, anon., c.1720. V&A: P.51–1962.*

In eighteenth-century Britain, women also took tea in tea gardens fitted with wooden alcoves and seats. However, many of these places became disreputable over time, and they were superseded during the following century by coffee houses, which also served tea. The clean and respectable tea rooms introduced in the 1860s were a further development, enabling unaccompanied women to

sit down and linger over the drink, served with or without a meal. Among the best known surviving tea rooms are those opened by Catherine Cranston in Glasgow from the 1870s, some of which have decoration by Charles Rennie Mackintosh (1868–1928; plate 67). The earlier seventeenth- and eighteenth-century coffee shops, which had served tea, coffee and other drinks, had been for men only.

The utensils required for the domestic service of tea during the eighteenth century were many and expensive, comprising, at the minimum, ceramic tea bowls or cups, saucers, canisters for different types of tea, a sugar basin, and a teapot and kettle. Many tea equipages also included a wooden, lacquer or ceramic tray, a hot-water pot, a jug for cream or milk, sugar tongs and a sugar knife (for cutting cane sugar), teaspoons, a spoon tray, a basin for dregs, a teapot stand, and one or more plates; by the end or the century a hot-water urn might also be required (plates 64, 65, 68, 69, 72, 74). The lady of the house would take a quantity of tea from one of the canisters with a pierced spoon and place it in the teapot; after filling the pot with freshly boiled water she would

allow the tea to draw. Until about 1720 silver teapots sometimes had a spirit lamp below to keep their contents warm.

The growing fashion for tea created a new demand for fine pottery and porcelain tea wares, prompting a succession of innovations in the European ceramic industries. Ceramic teapots, for example, became much more common from about 1740. It was from this time that the Staffordshire potters made extensive use of the slip-casting technique to reproduce complicated shapes in bulk. English ceramic factories immediately began introducing teapots in new and fantastic shapes, the novelty teapot having been revived periodically ever since (plate 71). Chinese decoration was long considered appropriate for ceramic teapots (plate 70) and other tea wares

70. *Chinoiserie teapot, soft-paste porcelain, Chelsea, 1745–7. V&A: C.46–1938.*

71. *Novelty teapot, earthenware, Burgess & Leigh, Burslem, Staffordshire, design registered 1896. V&A: C.278–1983.*

because of the East Asian origin of both porcelain and tea. From the 1770s, with the rise of neoclassicism, Chinese designs fell from fashion. As a French visitor to Britain commented in 1784, 'The drinking of tea… gives the rich an opportunity to show off their fine possessions: cups, teapots, etc., all made to the most elegant designs, all copies of the Etruscan and the antique.'[53]

Early tea canisters were frequently fitted with a lock, to prevent servants from pilfering; and until the end of the eighteenth century, when tea became much cheaper, they were often rather small. Only after about 1800 or 1820, when tea drinking was no longer the elitist pastime it had formerly been, were the canisters, kettle and other accessories banished to the kitchen, where tea was henceforward usually prepared. By this date

72. Canister for green tea, enamelled glass with gilt mounts and enamelled copper lid, West Midlands, England, 1755–60. V&A: 5288–1901.

73. Tea caddy, rolled paperwork and embroidery on wooden carcass, probably Long Melford, England, about 1800–30. V&A: W.31–1927.

tea canisters were known as 'caddies' in Britain, a term deriving from the Malay word for a weight equivalent to about half a kilogram, which is far more than could have been accommodated in the majority of these small boxes and jars (plates 69, 72, 73).

The earliest English and Dutch kettles were usually made of silver, as they were used in front of guests rather than being confined to the kitchen as they are in the West today. Early depictions of the English taking tea occasionally show a kettle of boiling water being brought from the kitchen by a turbaned black servant boy (plate 74). After about 1760 vase-shaped tea urns fitted with a tap came to replace kettles and hot-water jugs for replenishing teapots. The name 'tea urn' is misleading, as they contained water rather than tea. The water was kept hot by means of an iron bar that had been heated in a stove. Later, around 1800, when odourless fuels became available, models fitted with burners became popular (plate 75). Large caterers' urns of the type that dispense brewed tea were a later invention.

Teacups with handles began to be manufactured at Continental porcelain factories from about 1730 or 1740. Cups with handles had been made before this, but it is unclear whether or not they were used for tea. On the Continent the small cylindrical cups with handles generally called 'coffee cans' in Britain were not exclusively reserved for coffee, but were used more flexibly. Records of the Sèvres porcelain factory from the second half of the eighteenth century indicate that in France the same handled cups were used interchangeably for tea, coffee and chocolate.[54] Handled cups were more expensive to make and packed less efficiently than tea bowls during transport; in addition they may have been perceived as less authentically 'oriental' and less appropriate for tea at a time when the drink was still thought of in terms of its exotic Asian origins. For a variety of reasons, therefore, handleless bowls of the type imported from China and Japan remained popular until the early nineteenth century.

English paintings show that tea bowls could be held in a variety of different positions, none of them easy to maintain. Being able to handle a tea bowl with elegance and skill was an important social marker, indicating good breeding and worldly know-how. There are quite a number of eighteenth-century English and Dutch paintings of tea drinking, and it is indicative of the cost and important place of tea in the lives of the wealthy that they should have chosen to be commemorated in this way.

English satires and oil paintings of the late eighteenth and nineteenth centuries occasionally show tea being drunk from the saucer. While this was probably not acceptable in polite English company, tea may have been drunk in this way by the British in India, who had a very different climate to contend with (plate 76),[55] and also in eighteenth-century Scotland, Holland and France.[56] Writing in the 1670s or 1680s, the

76. The Dashwood and Auriol Familes, *oil on canvas, by Johann Zoffany, 1783–87. Reproduced with the kind permission of Robin Dashwood. Photograph by courtesy of the York Civic Trust.*

Dutch physician Cornelis Bontenkoe went so far as to claim that the flavour of tea could be enhanced by sipping it audibly.[57] In early eighteenth-century Britain, guests might indicate that they had had enough tea by turning over their cup and placing it on their saucer. Later in the century they did this by placing their teaspoon inside their empty cup.[58] Unless the appropriate signal had been made, it was considered bad manners to refuse a cup of tea when it was offered.

Until the nineteenth century, when tea was cultivated in India and Ceylon (Sri Lanka), most of the tea drunk in the West came from China. The Dutch had also imported tea from Japan during the seventeenth century, but in only modest quantities. The most popular type of black tea in eighteenth-century Britain was bohea, but other varieties such as pekoe, souchong and congou were also imported. Green teas included imperial hyson, gunpowder, and singlo or twankay. The British felt that green teas were more subtle in flavour than black, but that black teas tasted better with milk. By the mid-eighteenth century the English East India Company was importing strong black teas in far greater quantities than green, and following Britain's switch to teas from India and Ceylon in the nineteenth century green teas became rarer still. According to the *Grocer's Manual* of 1870, 'the green teas … so popular forty or fifty years ago are seldom heard of'.[59] In Holland, black teas became more popular than green varieties around 1750. The French, like the Chinese, frequently took their tea very weak, diluting a strong brew with water after pouring; judging from surviving French porcelain tea services from the middle of the eighteenth century, a small teapot might have been expected to provide sufficient tea for ten cups, or even, exceptionally, as many as 24.[60] Tea was also drunk far weaker in eighteenth-century Britain than is usual today.

Milk was often added to tea to counteract its bitter taste, much as with coffee and chocolate, and it may have been from these beverages that the habit of adding milk spread to tea. Although tea was described as

'prepared with milk and water' in Thomas Garway's advertisement of
about 1660, the European practice of taking tea with milk has been
claimed as a Parisian innovation of 1680.[61] Milk was not commonly
added to tea in England before the 1720s. Given that this was about the
date that black tea overtook green tea in popularity, there is a strong
likelihood that the two developments were connected. In late
seventeenth-century Holland it was fashionable to take green tea with
infused saffron, rather than milk;[62] and in eighteenth-century France tea
was often taken with lemon, as is still common today.

Sugar was commonly added to tea, coffee and chocolate from their
earliest appearances in both England and France, the Englishman Martin
Lister complaining in Paris in 1698 that these 'sugared liquors' resulted

in 'corpulency'.[63] The development of commercially viable sugar-refining processes from the 1650s paved the way for the West's adoption of these three drinks, all of which were considered unpalatably bitter on their own. Britain's sugar came from cane plantations in the West Indies, which led many to boycott sugar in protest against the slave trade during the years around 1800 (plate 78). The best sugar was refined and white: in 1784 a French visitor to England noted that 'Sugar, even unrefined sugar… is necessary [for tea] and very dear'.[64]

In eighteenth-century Holland tea was often followed by the serving of brandy and raisins. Similarly, cordials and spirits such as rum and brandy were commonly served after or alongside tea in eighteenth-century Britain, much as coffee is sometimes served alongside brandy in some western countries today. According to a woman's magazine of 1744, tea depressed the spirit and caused flatulency, faults that these alcoholic drinks could apparently counteract.[65]

Tea remained expensive throughout western Europe during the eighteenth century, though prices fell as the quantities imported increased. The English East India Company's imports rose dramatically during these years: £14,000 worth was imported in 1700; £179,000 in 1730; £969,000 in 1760; and £1,777,000 in 1790 (although some of this was re-exported to the American colonies). By the second half of the eighteenth century tea had come to form the single largest component in value of European trade with China. Naturally, such a successful item of commerce did not escape the notice of the British government, who introduced a specific tax on tea in 1698. Urged on by the breweries, this was periodically increased until the early 1780s, when it stood at 119 per cent of the price of the tea achieved at the East India Company's London auctions, thereby more than doubling its cost as it entered the wholesale market. The celebrated Boston Tea Party of 1773, when three shiploads of tea were dumped into Boston harbour, was triggered by the British government's attempts to impose its high duties on the tea re-exported

78. Anti-Saccharites, or John Bull … Leaving off the Use of Sugar, *etching, by James Gillray, 1792.* V&A: 15367.

to the American colonies. In view of these circumstances it is hardly surprising that large quantities of tea were smuggled into Britain, perhaps as much as half of Britain's annual consumption being illegally imported until taxes were cut in 1784. High retail prices also encouraged adulteration by unscrupulous merchants. Spent tea leaves, sloe leaves stained with liquorice, and even hawthorn or ash leaves boiled in sheep

TEE
TOTAL

dung were used to adulterate black teas; and some green teas contained tree leaves stained with verdigris or elder buds.

Despite these high prices, by the middle of the eighteenth century the British market for tea was widening, and the drink was no longer confined to the rich. Servants, for example, began to claim entitlement to an allowance of tea, and masters and mistresses who didn't oblige could expect their tea to be stolen. The spread of tea drinking to the lower classes was widely criticized, for three separate reasons. Firstly it took money away from other more basic needs. Secondly, many felt it was inappropriate for servants and the poor to be adopting the privileges of their masters. And thirdly, by drinking tea in preference to beer or ale, which were important sources of nourishment, the poor were exposing themselves to the risk of malnutrition. Today, we no doubt find it curious that moralists should have condemned tea drinking as improper and to have recommended alcoholic beverages instead. During the nineteenth and twentieth centuries this was of course reversed, tea being championed by members of the temperance movement from the 1820s onwards (plate 79).

Matters in Britain came to a crisis in the 1780s, when a series of bad harvests pushed the price of beer and ale beyond the reach of the poor. In response the government introduced the Commutation Act of 1784, which reduced import duties on tea from around 119 per cent to a mere 12.5 per cent. Prices immediately fell, and within a decade imports had quadrupled in volume. Writing in the year of the Act, a French visitor noted, 'The drinking of tea is general throughout England … even the humblest peasant will take his tea twice a day' [66] (plate 81). By the end of the century vast quantities of tea were being drunk by rich and poor alike. Further tax cuts followed in the 1860s, leading to lower prices still.

Tea had several other uses for eighteenth-century Britons, most of

81. A Cottage Interior with Poor Woman Preparing Tea, *oil on canvas, by W.R. Bigg (RA), 1793. V&A: 199–1885.*

which seem strange today. [67] For example, spent tea leaves could be used to clean carpets: they were scattered on the floor, allowed to soak up the dirt and then swept away. They were also spread on bread and butter and eaten lightly sugared, or served with an oil and vinegar dressing. Green tea leaves could be eaten 'neat': one letter writer of 1790 noted that young ladies were eating large quantities of 'neat green tea, with the greatest apparent relish', adding that it was '*exceedingly* pernicious when so taken'. Another diarist recorded how someone unfamiliar with the drink received a present of a pound of tea: she boiled the entire quantity in a kettle and served it with salt and butter, much to the disgust of her friends. The custom of reading or divining someone's future from the leaves left in their cup goes back at least as far as the 1720s.

During the early to mid-eighteenth century, wealthy Britons ate dinner, the main meal of the day, during daylight hours, often starting around two o'clock. By the end of the century, following improvements in artificial lighting, dinner was often eaten much later, around six or seven o'clock. In order to bridge the long gap between breakfast and dinner, a light accompaniment of bread and butter or toast, or biscuits or cakes, was sometimes served with mid-afternoon tea. By about 1840 this light snack had become the formal social event known as 'afternoon tea'. 'High tea' was a further nineteenth-century development in which tea was served together with a more substantial late afternoon meal of cold meat, sandwiches, pies and cakes. Initially a working-class custom, the convenience of high tea was such that it was adopted by the upper classes. Both high and afternoon tea survive in Britain today.

7

TEA AFTER 1900

ALUN GRAVES

'A Proper Tea is much nicer than a Very Nearly Tea,
which is one you forget about afterwards.'
A.A. MILNE, 1882–1956, *WINNIE THE POOH*

Tea after 1900

'Morning, Jeeves,' I said.

'Good morning, sir,' said Jeeves.

He put the good old cup of tea softly on the table by my bed, and I took a refreshing sip. Just right, as usual. Not too hot, not too sweet, not too weak, not too strong, not too much milk, and not a drop spilled in the saucer. A most amazing cove, Jeeves. So dashed competent in every respect... . He always floats in with the cup exactly two minutes after I come to life. Makes a deuce of a lot of difference to a fellow's day.

P.G. WODEHOUSE, *The Inimitable Jeeves*, 1923

COMIC THOUGH THEY MAY BE, Bertie Wooster's thoughts on the subject of his early morning cup of tea reflect the important position that the drink has occupied in the rhythms and rituals of daily life in Britain, and demonstrate the exacting demands of individual taste in the preparation of the brew. The early morning cup, a stimulant frequently enjoyed in bed, was the first of a number of occasions throughout the day when tea would typically be drunk. At the start of the twentieth century, these occasions were relatively clearly defined, following customs established in the previous century and governed to a considerable extent by class. Nowadays, however, the greater informality of people's lifestyles has resulted in a diminution of the rituals that once surrounded the taking of tea, and the intimate connections that formerly existed between tea drinking and the consumption of food have become severely eroded. While tea remains hugely popular, it is now less commonly seen as an appropriate mealtime drink.

Throughout the twentieth century the British were the world's greatest consumers of tea, and they remain so today.[68] Vast quantities have routinely been drunk at every level of the social scale. While only the rich may have been privileged enough to have their early morning tea brought to their bedside by a servant, the working classes of the early twentieth

(Previous pages) **82.** *Detail from plate 84.*

83. Afternoon Tea
*teapot, cup and
saucer, plate and
preserve pot,
bone china and
earthenware
(preserve pot),
designed by Eric
Ravilious and made
by Wedgwood &
Sons, Ltd.,
Staffordshire, 1937.
V&A: Circ.358–
359–1939, Circ.471
& 479–1948.*

century did at least enjoy the same drink to start their day. For them, tea would have provided a regular punctuation to their waking hours, being drunk at breakfast and along with other meals, as well as during breaks in the working day. Among the upper and middle classes too, tea was often drunk at breakfast, although coffee was generally more popular. Tea was less commonly consumed during the middle part of the day, although tea rooms increasingly catered to the requirements of shoppers and women in need of refreshment away from the home. The greatest ritual in the tea drinking day, however, remained that of afternoon tea (plates 82, 84).

Firmly established among the wealthier classes during the course of the nineteenth century, afternoon tea maintained its popularity well into the twentieth. Served between four and five o'clock and consisting of tea accompanied by cakes, pastries or biscuits, it provided a light filler to bridge the gap between lunch and a late dinner or supper (plate 83). Afternoon tea persisted as a relatively genteel affair, and was frequently used as a way of entertaining guests. It no longer remained, however, the sole preserve of the upper classes, and by the 1930s tea parties were being emulated further down the social scale.[69] Perhaps with this in mind, as well as in view of the changed circumstances in which the gentry increasingly found themselves, Elizabeth Craig advised readers of her handbook of entertaining, published in 1933, that the ideal was to 'entertain brightly without undue expenditure of either labour or money', and went on to offer a variety of suggestions for afternoon tea for the hostess without a maid.[70] Such a tea might include bread and butter, sandwiches, scones, toast, smoked salmon, biscuits, cakes and, she proposed, a choice of China tea served with lemon, or Darjeeling. For serving the tea, Craig recommended a tray laid with the necessary cups, saucers, tea caddy, cream jug, sugar bowl, slop basin, strainer, and plate of cut lemon.[71] Tea plates would be in a pile close by, with triangularly folded serviettes to one side. Once the tea was poured, a plate with a serviette placed on top was to be passed to each guest along with their cup and saucer. A 'nest' of tables, it was suggested, would provide convenient flat surfaces around the room. After two cups of tea had been poured for each guest, fresh tea was to be brewed, and if a maid was in attendance, she was to keep on replenishing the kettle to ensure a constant supply of hot water. Although they now sound quaintly formal, such arrangements were clearly seen as homely and intimate; they were contrasted, interestingly, with the serving of afternoon tea in the United States, which, it was noted, often involved illumination by 'a blaze of flickering candles'.

While the partaking of afternoon tea gradually filtered down to the middle classes, the more substantial high tea had, by the beginning of the twentieth century, worked its way up the social scale to become a widespread and increasingly respectable affair. Established during the previous century as the main evening meal of the working classes, high tea was generally served around six o'clock, after all the family had returned home. It had gained considerable popularity among the middle classes by the 1890s, Mrs Beeton reporting that in many homes it had taken the place of late dinner. She noted its particular popularity among the young, for whom it was a 'movable feast which can be partaken of at hours which will not interfere with tennis, boating or other amusements', and at which 'little formality is needed'.[72] The adoption of high tea at all levels of society marked the beginning of a trend towards informality that has continued up to the

84. Interior – The Orange Blind, *oil on canvas, by Francis C.B. Cadell, c.1927. Courtesy of Glasgow Museums: Art Gallery & Museum, Kelvingrove.*

present day. Tea may be less commonly drunk at mealtimes than it used to be, but the practice of eating at times and in ways that complement our leisure activities is one with which we are all familiar.

As well as being drunk at home and in the workplace, tea has increasingly been consumed in tea rooms and other public places. As with afternoon and high tea, this was a trend that began in the latter part of the nineteenth century and burgeoned in the twentieth. The firm of J. Lyons & Co. famously operated what was in the 1930s the largest chain of tea shops in the world, ranging from relatively small establishments to grand restaurants where orchestras would play. The tea was served by stylishly dressed waitresses known as 'nippies'. In London the Aerated Bread Company, or ABC, operated another large chain of tea shops, though these were rather more basic in style. Tea rooms were to be found throughout the country, with different chains operating in the different regions. In summer tea was often taken out of doors in tea gardens set up in parks and other public and private places. The increasing mobility afforded by cars and motorcycles, coupled with the ever growing popularity of outdoor pursuits, also made picnics commonplace (plate 85). At the start of the twentieth century, the hot water for the tea that would typically be drunk on such occasions was usually boiled on a spirit burner. Such arrangements were soon rendered unnecessary, however, by the increasing availability of the thermos, which went into commercial manufacture in the early 1900s.

The global popularity of tea drinking in the early twentieth century is reflected in the statistics compiled by William Ukers in his encyclopaedic study of tea published in 1935. At the top of Ukers' list of principal tea-drinking countries, which was ordered by *per capita* consumption, came the United Kingdom and Ireland,

85. *A group of women enjoying a picnic, possibly near Greenock, Renfrewshire, about 1900. Courtesy of The Trustees of the National Museums of Scotland.*

New Zealand, Australia, Canada and the Netherlands.[73] The European population of South Africa also drank relatively large quantities. Next in rank came the United States, Germany (plate 86) and France, where consumption was, however, substantially lower. The annual *per capita* amount of tea consumed in New Zealand and Australia was only a couple of pounds less than the nine or ten pounds (4–4.5kg) recorded for the United Kingdom. Among the various different ways of preparing infused tea noted by Ukers were the Australian bushman's 'billy can', in which water and tea were boiled together and allowed to stew for long periods of time, and the Canadian practice of decanting the tea into a second warmed teapot once it had been allowed to brew for the required length of time. The USA has also made its contribution to global tea culture by way of popularizing iced tea.

The modern preference in Britain and the tea-drinking countries of the Commonwealth has been for strong black teas. At the start of the twentieth century, this demand was largely met by teas from India and Ceylon (Sri Lanka). Since then plantations established in Africa in the early years of the twentieth century have helped meet demand, Kenya in particular having become a major exporter to Britain. The more delicate teas from China, which dominated imports until the late nineteenth century, served only a relatively small connoisseur market during the twentieth. While tea was formerly sold loose like coffee sometimes still is today, proprietary blends in conveniently sized packets became increasingly prevalent as the twentieth century progressed (plate 88). Advertising and clever marketing, in particular that of companies such as Brooke Bond and Ty-Phoo, was another important aspect of the growing commercialization of tea (plate 87). Brooke Bond's customer loyalty scheme for its 'dividend' tea, first retailed in 1935, was one of

86. *Poster designed by Ludwig Hohlwein, Germany, 1910. V&A: E.361–1921.*

87. *Poster issued by The Empire Tea Market Expansion Bureau, Britain, 1939. V&A: E.128–1973.*

88. *A range of packeted tea produced by R. Twining & Co., as illustrated in their wholesale price list, about 1937. V&A: TLC.1.793.*

many such schemes that have been launched over the years. Up until the Second World War, more exclusive purveyors such as Twinings also maintained a substantial direct trade with wealthy families who ran houses with large numbers of staff. Surviving records show that customers like these ordered between 25 and 100 pounds (11–45kg) of tea at a time.[74]

The two world wars had a considerable impact on the availability of tea in Britain. Although during the First World War tea was not rationed like many other staple foodstuffs, for a five-month period during 1918 its distribution was controlled by a system of national registration based on an allocation of two ounces (56g) per person per week. The importance attached to tea by the British government is reflected in the measures it took at the outbreak of the Second World War to move the stocks of tea in bonded warehouses along the River

Thames to safer locations around the country, away from the risk of air raids. The ensuing confusion over ownership led the government to buy up all the tea on the books of dealers and merchants, and to make weekly allocations back to them. Rationing was introduced in July 1940. Initially the allowance was two ounces (56g) of tea per person per week, but it was increased to up to two-and-a-half ounces (70g) when stocks permitted. Sugar was also rationed and tended to be in very short supply. The need to conserve what little was available for other purposes, such as the preserving of fruit, prompted many people to go without sugar in their tea for the first time. In many cases this habit remained even after the de-rationing of tea in 1952.[75]

The range of equipment used in the preparation and serving of tea gradually evolved during the twentieth century, reflecting technological innovation and cultural change. Edwardian tea services were essentially the same as those of the Victorian period. The most costly were of silver or bone china. Pewter, as previously, was a cheaper alternative (plate 89), as was earthenware. While the basic composition of the tea service remained essentially unchanged, during the 1930s progressive manufacturers such as the Susie Cooper Pottery began to produce smaller, more practical services suited to the needs of modern lifestyles. Standard earthenware tea services were sold with six cups and saucers. Also on offer were newer combinations such as the 'tea-for-two', which was particularly suited to early morning use. Since the Second World War stainless steel has been used for the manufacture both of 'designer' tea services (plate 90) and of mass-produced vessels of the sort ubiquitously found in cafés and restaurants. Teapots have been particularly subject to design experimentation, though rarely with any lasting results. More successful designs include the 'cube' tea set, originally produced around 1916 for use on ocean liners, which

89. *Tudric tea set, pewter, designed by Archibald Knox and made by W.H. Haseler, Birmingham, for Liberty & Co., 1903– 4. V&A: Circ.915–918– 1967.*

90. Alverston *tea set, stainless steel, designed by Robert Welch and made by J.J. Wiggin Ltd, Walsall, for Old Hall Tableware Ltd, 1962. V&A: M.19–1978.*

cleverly compressed the teapot, jug and sugar bowl into cubes that could be fitted snugly together (plate 91). A practical innovation of the 1930s was the insulated teapot, which kept its contents hot by means of a lagged chrome casing. More fancifully, novelty teapots have been made in the shape of virtually everything imaginable. Despite these many variations, however, rarely have the teapot's basic features of body, handle, spout and lid been challenged in any serious way; and, perhaps unsurprisingly, it has been the simplest, most practical designs that have been the most enduring (plate 93). The centrality of the teapot's place in ceramic history has also made it a favourite vehicle for exploration by modern craft potters, for whom complexity of construction and the demands of functionality present particular challenges (plate 92).

Methods of tea preparation also underwent extensive changes in the twentieth century. One technological development that had a major impact was the arrival of electricity in the home. Prior to this, water had to be boiled on a stove or fire, or else heated with a portable spirit burner (plate 94). With the advent of the electric kettle, however, water could be boiled quickly and conveniently (plate 95). Electric kettles are now standard in British homes, though stove-top models remain popular elsewhere in Europe (plate 96). Perhaps the most significant development in modern tea culture, however, has been

DENBY
OVEN AND TABLE WARE

*In addition to the standard brown finish Denby ware
is now available in two attractive colours — Manor Green and Cottage Blue.*

JOSEPH BOURNE & SON LTD · DENBY POTTERY · NEAR DERBY

91. *Cube tea set,
earthenware, made
by George Clews
& Co. Ltd, Tunstall,
Staffordshire,
about 1936.
V&A: C.150–1977.*

92. *Tea Cabaret Set,
earthenware, by
Morgen Hall, 1997.
V&A: C.9–16–1998.*

93. Cottage Blue *tea
set, stoneware, made
by Joseph Bourne and
Son, Ltd at the Denby
Pottery, Derbyshire,
1926 onwards, as
illustrated in a
company leaflet.
Reproduced from
I. & G. Hopwood,
Denby Pottery
1809–1997, 1997.*

the tea bag. In use in the United States since the 1920s, the tea bag has made the process of infusing tea supremely clean and easy. Initially confined to public eating places, tea bags became increasingly popular in American homes during the 1930s. They took longer to gain acceptance in Britain, however, and it is only since the 1960s that they have been commonplace. Today, around 90 per cent of the tea consumed in Britain is made with tea bags. This has inevitably had an impact on the equipment used for making tea. Firstly, because tea can be brewed directly in the cup, the teapot has been rendered less essential than it used to be. Secondly, and perhaps more significantly, because traditional cups and saucers are too small to use with tea bags, or are considered too formal, mugs, which were formerly reserved for use by workmen or in canteens, have gained respectability and are now the standard vessel from which most people drink tea in the home.

Tea remains the United Kingdom's favourite drink. Some 165 million cups of tea were consumed each day in the mid-1990s, accounting for almost 4 per cent of all drinks consumed.[76] The competition from coffee has increased steadily over the years, but the amount consumed is still only half that of tea. An increasingly health-conscious public are also becoming aware of the medicinal benefits of tea, which recent research suggests has a role to play in the prevention of heart disease and cancer. The future for tea is bright and its continued popularity seems assured.

96. *Kettle, stainless steel, designed by Michael Graves and made by Alessi SpA, Milan, 1985. V&A: M.11–1990.*

Further reading

Algar, A.E., *The Complete Book of Turkish Cookery*, London,1985

Balland, D., and Bazin, M., 'Cay –'Tea', in *Encyclopaedia Iranica*, California, 1992, pp.103–7

Bell, C., *The People of Tibet*, New Delhi, 1928 (reprinted 1991)

Brown, P., *In Praise of Hot Liquors*, York, 1995

Brussels, Galerie du Crédit Communal, *Tea for 2: Les Rituels de Thé dans la Monde*, 1999

Chamberlain, L., *The Food and Cookery of Russia*, London, 1982

Combe, G.A., *A Tibetan on Tibet*, Kathmandu, 1926 (reprinted 1975)

Craig, E., *Entertaining with Elizabeth Craig*, London, 1933

Davies, J., *The Wartime Kitchen and Garden*, London, 1993

Day, I. (ed.), *Eat, Drink and Be Merry: The British at Table, 1600–2000*, London, 2000

Emmerson, R., *British Teapots and Tea Drinking*, London, 1992

Faroqhi, S., *Subjects of the Sultan: Culture and Daily Life in the Ottoman Empire*, London, 2000

Fujioka, R. (trans. L.A. Cort), *Tea Ceremony Utensils*, New York, 1973

Graham, P.J., *Tea of the Sages: The Art of Sencha*, Honolulu, 1998

Guth, C., *Art, Tea and Industry: Masuda Takashi and the Mitsui Circle*, Princeton, 1993

Hann, C., *Tea and Domestication of the Turkish State*, London, 1990

Harrer, H., *Lost Lhasa*, New York, 1992

Hobhouse, H., *Seeds of Change*, London, 1985

Hong Kong Museum of Art, *Chinese Ceramic Tea Vessels*, Hong Kong, 1991

Lo, K.S., *The Stonewares of Yixing from the Ming Period to the Present Day*, Hong Kong, 1986

Lu Yu (trans. F.R. Carpenter), *Chajing (Classic of Tea)*, Boston and Toronto, 1974

Matthee, R., 'From Coffee to Tea: Shifting Patterns of Consumption in Qajar Iran', *Journal of World History*, vol.2 no.2, 1996, pp.199–230

Migot, A., *Tibetan Marches*, London, 1955

Mowry, R.D., *Hare's Fur, Tortoiseshell, and Partridge Feathers: Chinese Brown- and Black-Glazed Ceramics 400–1400*, Cambridge (Massachusetts), 1996

Okakura, K., *The Book of Tea*, New York, 1906

Papashvily, H. & G., *Russian Cooking*, New York, 1969

Pettigrew, J., *A Social History of Tea*, London, 2001

Rockhill, W.W., *Land of the Lamas*, Washington, 1891

Rockhill, W.W., *Diary of a Journey through Mongolia and Tibet in 1891 and 1892*, Washington, 1894

Sen, S. *et al.*, *The Japanese Way of Tea: From its Origins in China to Sen Rikyū*, Honolulu, 1998

Shaida, M., *The Legendary Cuisine of Persia*, London, 1992

Spencer Chapman, F., *Lhasa the Holy City*, London, 1940

Tanaka, S., *The Tea Ceremony*, Tokyo, 1973

Tapper, R. and Zubaida, S. (eds.), *Culinary Cultures of the Middle East*, London, 1994

Twining, S.H., *The House of Twining*, London, 1956

Ukers, W.H., *All about Tea*, 2 vols., New York, 1935

Varley, P. and Kumakura, I. (eds.), *Tea in Japan: Essays on the History of Chanoyu*, Honolulu, 1989

Waddell, A., *Lhasa and its Mysteries*, London, 1906

Notes

1 Ukers (1935), vol.II, p.316.

2 *Zhou Li*, chapter Di Guan (*Rituals of the Zhou Dynasty*, chapter 'Earthly Officials'), Part II.

3 Zhang Yi, *Guang Ya* (a glossary compiled in the third century), says 'In the Hunan and Sichuan areas tea is collected and made into cakes … the resulting beverage drives away intoxication from alcohol'. In *Taiping Yulan*, an encyclopaedia compiled in 977, chapter 867.

4 Lu Yu, *Chajing*, written about 758, annotated by Zhou Jingmin in *Zhongguo Cha Jiu Cidian* (*Dictionary of Chinese Tea and Wine*), Hunan Press, 1992. The passages quoted are not direct translations but rather excerpts from chapters 4, 5 and 6.

5 Zhao Ruli, *Beiyuan Bielu* (*Supplementary Notes from the North Garden*), written in 1186, p.1.

6 Wu Zimu, *Meng Liang Lu* (*Dreams of the Old Days*), written in the 1270s, chapter 16, Shanghai Guji reprint, 1956, p.262.

7 Cai Xiang, *Cha Lu* (*Record of Tea*), written in 1051, Part I.

8 Cheng Dachang, *Yan Fanlu*, written in the twelfth century, chapter 15.

9 A Yixing teapot is among the grave goods in the tomb of a eunuch who died in 1533. See Liang Baiquan, *Yixing Purple Clay Ware*, Hong Kong, 1991, p.44. In the Flagstaff House Museum of Teaware, Hong Kong, is a Yixing teapot dated 1513. See Lo (1986), p.52.

10 Wen Zhenheng, *Zhang Wu Zhi* (*Superfluous Things*), written about 1600–40, chapter 12.

11 *ibid.*

12 A vivid description can be found in the satirical novel *Guanchang Xianxing Ji* (*Truths about Officialdom*), written in 1901–3, Taipei Sanmin Shuju reprint, 1979, pp.17–18.

13 Xu Ke, *Qing Bai Lei Chao* (*Qing Dynasty Unofficial Records by Category*), compiled in 1916, vol. 47 (Eating and Drinking), Commercial Press, n.d., p.109.

14 Kaempfer, E. (trans. J.G. Scheuchzer), *History of Japan*, London, 1727, vol.II, Appendix, p.15.

15 *ibid.*, vol. I, capter IX, p.115.

16 For early developments in Japanese tea drinking see Graham (1998), pp.10–16, and Murai Yasuhiko, 'The Development of *Chanoyu* before Rikyū', in Varley and Kumakura (1989), pp.3–32.

17 For depictions of different methods of tea preparation as seen in Edo period woodblock prints and illustrated books see Iruma City Museum, *Ocha to Ukiyo-e* (*Tea and Ukiyo-e*), Iruma, 1997.

18 For *senchadō* and Japanese steeped tea drinking more generally see Graham (1998).

19 Beckwith, C.I., 'Tibet and the Early Medieval Florissance in Eurasia', *Central Asiatic Journal*, 1977, vol.21, p.100.

20 Rosthorn, A. von, *On Tea Cultivation in West Sichuan and the Tea Trade with Tibet via Tachienlu*, London, 1895, pp.13–14.

21 Waddell (1906), p.477.

22 Bell (1928; reprinted 1991), p.122.

23 Grenard, F., *Tibet, the Country and its Inhabitants*, London, 1894, p.294.

24 For the tea trade see Rockhill (1891), pp.279–84; Rockhill (1894), p.119; *op. cit.* Rosthorn (1895), pp.26–7, 32; Burrard, G., *Records of the Survey of India*, vol. 8, part 2, Dehra Dun, *c*.1880, pp.233–5; Waddell (1906), pp.353, 477–8; Bell (1928; reprinted 1991), p.121; Migot (1955), pp.89, 142; and Spengen, W. van, 'The Geo-History of Long-Distance Trade in Tibet 1850–1950', *Tibet Journal*, vol.20 no.2, Summer 1995, pp.18–63.

25 Rockhill (1894), p.119.

26 For the preparation and making of tea in Tibet see Combe (1926; reprinted 1975), pp.132–3; Bell (1928; reprinted 1991), pp.236–7; Spencer Chapman (1940), p.52; and Harrer (1992), pp.114–17.

27 Olson, E., *Catalogue of the Tibetan Collection in the Newark Museum*, vol.5, Newark, 1971, p.3.

28 Harrer (1992), pp.114–17.

29 For dragon-handled teapots see Clarke, J., 'Chiling, a Village of Ladakhi Craftsmen and their Products', *Arts of Asia*, May/June 1989, pp.128–41, and Clarke, J., 'Regional Styles of Metalwork', in Singer, J. and Denwood, P., *Tibetan Art:*

Towards a Definition of Style, London, 1997, pp.278–89.

[30] For tea bowls see Rockhill (1891), p.341, and Bell (1928; reprinted 1991), pp.128, 240.

[31] Rockhill (1891), p.293.

[32] Baddeley, R., *Russia, Mongolia, China*, London, 1919, vol.2, p.118.

[33] Ukers (1935), vol.I, p.32.

[34] Richardson, W., *Anecdotes of the Russian Empire*, London, 1784, cited in Kelly, L., *St Petersburg: A Travellers' Companion*, London, 1981, p.235.

[35] Smith, R., 'Whence the Samovar', *Petit Propos Culinaire*, vol.4, 1980, p.63.

[36] A gold and silver samovar made in 1866 for Tsarevich Alexander (later Alexander III) and inscribed with his name is illustrated in Papashvily (1969), p.9.

[37] Karsavina, T., *Theatre Street*, London, 1930, p.76.

[38] Sykes, E., *Persia and its People*, London, 1910, p.98.

[39] Olearius, A., *Vermehrte newe Beschreibung der Muscowitischen und Persischen Reyse*, Schleswig, 1656, p.599.

[40] Kaempfer, E., *Die Reisetagbucher Engelbert Kaempfers*, 1684–5, cited in Matthee (1996), p.203.

[41] Jaubert, P.A., *Voyage en Armenie et en Perse fait dans les Années 1805 et 1806*, Paris, 1821, p.206.

[42] Wulff, H., *The Traditional Crafts of Persia*, Cambridge, 1966, pp.28–30.

[43] Sheil, Lady, *Glimpses of Life and Manners in Persia*, London, 1856, p.133.

[44] Celebi, E. (van Bruinessen, M., trans. and ed.), *Evliya Celebi in Diyarbekir*, Leiden, 1988, p.170.

[45] The following works have proved especially useful in writing this chapter: Ukers (1935), Emmerson (1992) and Brown (1995). Pettigrew (2001) contains useful information on tea drinking in nineteenth-century Britain, and Savill, R., *The Wallace Collection: Catalogue of Sèvres Porcelain*, London, 1988, on tea in eighteenth-century France.

[46] Ukers (1935), vol.I, p.23 and Brown (1995), pp.4 and 6, quoting Giambattista Ramusio, *Navigatione e Viaggi*, 1559.

[47] Ukers (1935), vol.I, p.23, and Brown (1995), p.31.

[48] Ukers (1935), vol.I, p.33, quoting Father Alexander of Rhodes.

[49] Jorge Tavares da Silva, 'Catarina de Bragança, The Tea Drinking Queen?', in Brussels (1999), pp.15–27.

[50] Ukers (1935), vol.I, p.44.

[51] Emmerson (1992), p.4.

[52] *The Female Spectator*, cited in Berg, M., and Clifford, H. (eds.), *Consumers and Luxury*, Manchester, 1999, p.161.

[53] Emmerson (1992), p.14, quoting François, Duc de La Rochefoucauld.

[54] *op. cit.* Savill (1988), p.489.

[55] Emmerson (1992), p.19.

[56] See Ukers (1935), vol.II, pp.401 and 403, and *op. cit.* Savill, 1988, p.489 respectively.

[57] Scheuleer, T.H.L., 'The Dutch at Tea-Table', *Connoisseur*, October 1976, p.90.

[58] Ukers (1935), vol.II, p.403 and Emmerson (1992), p.23.

[59] Pettigrew (2001), p.97.

[60] *op. cit.* Savill (1988), p.490.

[61] Ukers (1935), vol.I, p.35, where attributed to Mme de la Sablière.

[62] Ukers (1935), vol.II, p. 401.

[63] Brown (1995), p.42.

[64] Emmerson (1992), p.11, quoting François, Duc de La Rochefoucauld.

[65] *The Female Spectator*, cited in Charleston, R.J., *English Glass and the Glass Used in England, c.400–1940*, London, 1984, p.161.

[66] Emmerson (1992), p.11, quoting François, Duc de La Rochefoucauld.

[67] All instances here are taken from Warner, O., *The English Teapot*, London, 1948, pp.4–5, and Ukers (1935), vol.II, p.404.

[68] Ukers (1935), vol.II, p.409.

[69] From a survey conducted by Sir William Crawford and Herbert Broadley in 1938, and reported in Pettigrew (2001), p.161.

[70] Craig (1933), pp.iii and 16.

[71] Craig (1933), pp.128–9.

[72] Day (2000), pp.120–21.

[73] Ukers (1935), vol.II, p.349.

[74] Twining (1956), p.87.

[75] Davies (1993), pp.69–70.

[76] Data from the Tea Council website.

Index

figures in italics indicate illustrations